WHEN THE WORLD STOPS

WHEN THE WORLD STOPS

MICHAEL L. BROWN, PhD

Visit the author's website at askdrbrown.org/, www.
booksbydrbrown.com.

Library of Congress Cataloging-in-Publication Data:
An application to register this book for cataloging has
been submitted to the Library of Congress.
International Standard Book Number: 978-1-62999-898-5
E-book ISBN: 978-1-62999-899-2

20 21 22 23 24 — 9 8 7 6 5 4 3 2 1
Printed in the United States of America

TABLE OF CONTENTS

PREFACE

WHEN I FIRST heard about a new virus strain in Wuhan, China, I paid little attention to it. What was the big deal? Very quickly, however, it became clear that this *was* a big deal. It also became clear very quickly that the reports of a potential pandemic sent waves of fear around the world, including within the church. There was panic. There was dread. And there were questions, lots of questions.

Was this virus man-made? Was it a bioweapon? Was it part of a one-world government takeover? Was it sent by the devil to destroy? Was it judgment from God? Was it one of the plagues in the Book of Revelation, signaling the end of the world?

I felt the need to begin addressing some of the

biblically based questions and to respond to the fears of God's people, writing my first relevant article on March 2, 2020, titled "Is the Coronavirus an End-Time Biblical Plague?"[1] In the days that followed, I preached on related themes, devoted radio broadcasts to similar themes (including one show where I went through Psalm 91 in Hebrew), and did livestreams on social media.

Then, on Wednesday, March 18, I sent an email to Steve Strang, Marcos Perez, and Kyle Duncan, my colleagues at Charisma Media, titled "Crazy Idea?" and suggested I put together a short book for immediate release in the midst of the crisis. Marcos wrote back immediately, saying, "Your email confirms a prompting I sensed yesterday while on vacation." Kyle wrote, "I want to just echo what Marcos has said, Dr. Brown. I think this is a fantastic idea." Eight days later, on March 26, with God's grace and help, I finished the manuscript—basically completing the book in one week.

My appreciation goes to the entire team at Charisma for grabbing hold of this vision and turning it around so quickly for the general public. (How often have you heard of a book being *written and published* in less than a month, from beginning to end?) And my appreciation goes to the many friends and prayer warriors who intercede for me and my ministry. Without them none of this would take place.

It is my prayer that as you read this book, God's peace and strength and wisdom will flood your heart, giving you courage and faith to stand strong, shining like a beacon of light and hope in dark and dangerous times. And while this book has been written against the backdrop of the coronavirus, it will be relevant in all times of crisis. One day the whole world will be shaken—but the righteous will never be shaken. May it be so!

One quick request: If this book is a blessing to you, tell a friend, and then post a short review on Amazon. And if you don't receive regular updates and important news from our ministry, please connect with us at AskDrBrown.org. We would love to stay in touch and be an ongoing blessing in your life.

—MICHAEL L. BROWN
MARCH 27, 2020

Chapter One

FEAR NOT!

WE ARE LIVING in unprecedented times, and it's easy to give way to fear. After all, the news reports are daunting, and the scientific predictions, terrifying. As I write this, whole countries are in lockdown and counties across America are telling people not to leave their homes. Schools have closed, businesses are shutting down, and the media is shouting through the airwaves, "Danger! The virus is coming your way!"

In a single day in Italy almost one thousand people died of COVID-19. A single extended family in New Jersey lost four family members to the virus, with three more hospitalized. From a single wedding party in Australia thirty-seven people tested positive. In a single nursing home in New Jersey, all ninety-four people were presumed to have the virus. And we've been told it will get worse before it gets better. How can we not be afraid?

One report offers what it calls "the grimmest version of life a year from now,"[1] meaning the worst prediction of where we could find ourselves one year from now. According to this worst-case scenario, in a year things could look like this:

> More than two million Americans have died from the new coronavirus, almost all mourned without funerals. Countless others have died because hospitals are too overwhelmed to deal adequately with heart attacks, asthma and diabetic crises. The economy has cratered into a depression, for fiscal and monetary policy are ineffective when people fear going out, businesses are closed and tens of millions of people are unemployed. A vaccine still seems far off, immunity among those who have recovered proves fleeting and the coronavirus has joined the seasonal flu as a recurring peril.[2]

Dr. Brian Monahan, the attending physician of Congress and the US Supreme Court, thinks matters could be even worse—much worse. He believes that as much as 50 percent of all Americans could get infected,[3] and if one in one hundred die, then *fifteen million Americans would die of the coronavirus.*

In countries like Italy, cemeteries are closed and caskets are lined up in rows. Even the crematoria are running at full capacity and beyond. *Italy cannot even burn its dead quickly enough.* How can we not be afraid?

A *Business Insider* story from March 20 painted a harrowing picture:

- Most of the city's public services are in crisis.

- On Wednesday night, fifteen Italian military trucks were seen ferrying about sixty bodies from morgues across the city to cremation sites in twelve other northern Italian cities after Bergamo's mayor called for aid.

- Several morgues and Bergamo's sole crematorium, which can cremate twenty-five people a day, are overwhelmed.

- Prohibited from holding services, churches have been used to store coffins. The gymnasium at Ponte San Pietro Hospital was turned into a makeshift mortuary.[4]

The truth be told, without the Lord it would be very easy to give place to fear. What will happen to my loved ones? What will happen to me? Who will die next? What about my job? How can I pay my rent (or mortgage)? How can I feed my family? What does the future hold? Does anyone know?

The good news is that with the Lord there is no place for fear. He is not rattled. He is not surprised. He is not taken off guard. He is not in a panic. To the contrary, He is working actively in the midst of the crisis, and He has a great plan for His people in the midst of the storm. God is on the move! And He is with us.

That's why the first message that has been sounding from pulpits across America is, "Fear not!" And that is the first message He wants to speak to each of our hearts—that is, if we are His children, in right relationship with Him. "Fear not," He says to us, "because I am with you."

That is all we need to know. If the Lord Himself, the Creator of the entire universe, is with us, we need not fear an epidemic or a pandemic. We need not fear demons or people. We need not fear the natural or the supernatural. If we have a healthy, reverential fear of the Lord, then all other fears will vanish. "Fear not!" the Lord says to you and me.

To the Jewish people in Babylonian captivity God said, "So do not fear, for I am with you; do not be dismayed, for I am your God. I will strengthen you and help you; I will uphold you with my righteous right hand" (Isa. 41:10). He speaks these same words to us today as we lean on Him and put our trust in His goodness, power, and wisdom. Can you say out loud with me, "Father, I put my trust in You"?

He also spoke this word to His people in captivity:

> But now, this is what the LORD says—he who created you, Jacob, he who formed you, Israel: "Do not fear, for I have redeemed you; I have summoned you by name; you are mine. When you pass through the waters, I will be with you; and when you pass through the rivers, they will not sweep over you. When you walk through the fire, you will not be burned; the flames will not set you ablaze."
>
> —ISAIAH 43:1–2

Do you see what our God is saying? We *will* experience difficult times. We *will* pass through water and fire. But we will not drown. We will not be burned. We will be protected through the storm because God is with us. That is why we do not fear.

The disciples didn't understand this. They were in a boat with Jesus, and He had fallen asleep while a terrible storm was raging. "We're going to die," they thought, "and He doesn't even care. He's sound asleep while we're struggling to keep the ship afloat."

As Mark records,

A furious squall came up, and the waves
broke over the boat, so that it was nearly
swamped. Jesus was in the stern, sleeping
on a cushion. The disciples woke him and
said to him, "Teacher, don't you care if we
drown?" He got up, rebuked the wind and
said to the waves, "Quiet! Be still!" Then the
wind died down and it was completely calm.
He said to his disciples, "Why are you so
afraid? Do you still have no faith?"

—MARK 4:37–40

There's a lesson to learn from this. Sometimes
we will go through serious storms. Sometimes the
water will get into the boat. Sometimes the winds
and the waves will be terrifying. And Jesus, it would
seem, is sound asleep, not aware of the trouble and
not lifting a finger to help. But that is only how it
appears. As long as Jesus is in your boat, you have
no reason to fear. He can control the weather. He
can still the storm with a single word from His lips.
That's why fear is a symptom of unbelief.

Can you put your faith in Jesus afresh right now?
Can you say to Him, "Lord, I will trust You and worship You and praise You, even in the midst of the
storm, even as the wind and waves come crashing
in on me. I will put my trust in You"? Can you do
that? Soon He will speak peace to the chaos. Until
then, He will speak peace to your heart.

All of us probably know Psalm 23; many of us

have it memorized. But have we really thought about what it means? Look carefully at verse 4, which says, "Even though I walk through the darkest valley, I will fear no evil, for you are with me; your rod and your staff, they comfort me." Yes, even though you and I walk through the darkest valley (traditionally translated "the valley of the shadow of death"), we have no reason for fear, *because God, our Shepherd, is with us.* As rendered in the NET, "Even when I must walk through the darkest valley, I fear no danger, for you are with me; your rod and your staff reassure me."

The truth be told, the valley itself is ominous. It is deep, dark, and full of dangers. But the only concern of each sheep is that the Shepherd is nearby, rod and staff in hand. He will beat off the enemies. He will protect us from every attack. No wolf or lion or other menacing predator can touch us. He is with us!

Jesus gave His disciples similar assurances shortly before His death and resurrection. They were about to pass through hellish times. They would watch their Master suffer terribly. They would see Him hanging on a cross and watch Him breathe His last breath. They would see their dreams and hopes shattered to pieces—at least that's how things would appear.

Yet He said to them, "Peace I leave with you; my peace I give you. I do not give to you as the world

gives. Do not let your hearts be troubled and do not
be afraid" (John 14:27). And He said this: "I have
told you these things, so that in me you may have
peace. In this world you will have trouble. But take
heart! I have overcome the world" (John 16:33).

Yes, in this world we *will* have trouble, be it from
people or from demons or from nature or from our
own poor choices. We live in a fallen world, and it
is a world marked by trouble. Yet in Jesus we have
peace. He has overcome it all, and in Him we too
overcome. Therefore, we do not fear. Instead, we
rejoice. He is with us!

That's why the Lord said to His disciples earlier in
His ministry, "Do not be afraid, little flock, for your
Father has been pleased to give you the kingdom"
(Luke 12:32). In the end we will be blessed beyond
our wildest dreams. In the here and now His goodness and love and guidance and provision will sustain us. In and through Him we can thrive in the
midst of the storm, and everything Satan or the
world means for evil can be turned for greater good.
He is with us!

The Gospels record the account of the resurrection of the daughter of Jairus. She was very ill, and
Jesus was coming to heal her, but before He could
arrive, the twelve-year-old girl had died. It was all
over, and nothing could be done. There was no more
need to trouble the Master—at least that's what

people thought. Instead, Jesus replied, "Do not fear; only believe, and she will be well" (Luke 8:50, ESV).

The words are so simple and clear: "Fear not; only believe, and your dead daughter will recover." You must simply believe—and believe only. This shows us that faith and fear are polar opposite forces. As Smith Wigglesworth said, "Fear looks; faith jumps." It's true! We could also say that:

- Fear paralyzes; faith liberates.

- Fear brings death; faith brings life.

- Fear brings torment; faith brings peace.

- Fear listens to the devil's lies; faith listens to God's truth.

- While fear is irrational, faith is rational.

- While fear is natural, faith is supernatural.

- Fear looks at earthly circumstances and anticipates worst-case scenarios; faith looks at God's promises and anticipates ultimate victories.

- Fear is fundamentally a denial of the existence of the God of the Bible; faith is founded on who He is and what He does.

God says to us today, "Fear not, only believe, and all will be well." He might stop the storm. He might give us grace to endure the storm. He might teach us patience. Or faith. Or perseverance. He might do something so out of the box that we can't even imagine it now. But of this we can be sure: Whether we live or die, He will be with us. Whether we go through easy times or hard times, His grace is sufficient. Therefore, we do not fear.

Psalm 46 says it so well. Read it slowly, and drink in every word (from the ESV):

> God is our refuge and strength, a very present help in trouble. Therefore we will not fear though the earth gives way, though the mountains be moved into the heart of the sea, though its waters roar and foam, though the mountains tremble at its swelling. *Selah*
>
> There is a river whose streams make glad the city of God, the holy habitation of the Most High. God is in the midst of her; she shall not be moved; God will help her when morning dawns. The nations rage, the kingdoms totter; he utters his voice, the earth melts. The LORD of hosts is with us; the God of Jacob is our fortress. *Selah*
>
> Come, behold the works of the LORD, how he has brought desolations on the earth. He makes wars cease to the end of the earth;

he breaks the bow and shatters the spear; he burns the chariots with fire. "Be still, and know that I am God. I will be exalted among the nations, I will be exalted in the earth!" The LORD of hosts is with us; the God of Jacob is our fortress. *Selah*

What a vivid picture. The earth might reel. The world might shake. The mountains might be cast into the sea. And still we will not fear, *because God is with us*. And so He says to each of us in the midst of the current crisis, "Be still, and know that I am God; I will be exalted among the nations, I will be exalted in the earth" (Ps. 46:10).

Do you hear His voice speaking to you now? Take hold of His words and be at peace. He is God—your God. There is no reason to fear. And regardless of what the future holds, He will be exalted. Put your trust in Him.

Chapter Two

FEED YOUR FAITH, NOT YOUR FEARS

S O HOW EXACTLY do we learn to "fear not"? How do we conquer our worries and our anxieties? What are some practical steps we can take? And what should we do if there is good reason to fear, such as being told that a category 5 hurricane is coming our way and there's no time to evacuate? Fear would seem like the right response!

In the previous chapter we saw that a major key to overcoming fear is to know that God Himself is with us, be it in a hurricane or a pandemic. That alone can produce supernatural peace and calm. In fact, the peace and calm can be so supernatural that others will notice it too.

John Wesley tells the story of his encounter with Moravian Christians who had a real relationship with God while at that time, he was deeply devoted to Christianity but didn't truly know the Lord. He had not yet been born again. And so after sailing from England to America to convert the "heathen," he returned home wondering, "Who shall convert me?"[1]

This was one of the events that so deeply impacted him, and he journaled about it on Sunday, January 25, 1736. He was sailing to America in the midst of a terrible storm, and he noticed that the Moravian Christians, whom he calls "the Germans," were not in a panic.

> At seven I went to the Germans. I had long before observed the great seriousness of their behaviour. Of their humility they had given a continual proof, by performing those servile offices for the other passengers, which none of the English would undertake; for which they desired, and would receive no pay, saying, "it was good for their proud hearts," and "their loving Saviour had done more for them." And every day had given them occasion of showing a meekness which no injury could move. If they were pushed, struck, or thrown down, they rose again and went away; but no complaint was found in their mouth. There was now an

opportunity of trying whether they were
delivered from the Spirit of fear, as well
as from that of pride, anger, and revenge.
In the midst of the psalm wherewith their
service began, the sea broke over, split the
main-sail in pieces, covered the ship, and
poured in between the decks, as if the great
deep had already swallowed us up. A terrible screaming began among the English.
The Germans calmly sung on. I asked one of
them afterwards, "Was you not afraid?" He
answered, "I thank God, no." I asked, "But
were not your women and children afraid?"
He replied, mildly, "No; our women and
children are not afraid to die."

From them I went to their crying, trem-
bling neighbours, and pointed out to them
the difference in the hour of trial, between
him that feareth God, and him that feareth
him not. At twelve the wind fell. This was
the most glorious day which I have hitherto
seen.[2]

God can give you His peace in the midst of the
storm—even a violent storm in which the sea breaks
over the ship, the mainsail is split in pieces, and it
looks as if the whole boat is about to be swallowed
by the ocean, killing everyone on board. That is a
real storm! Yet even then God's people can worship

and praise Him. His presence makes a massive, tangible difference.

There are also practical steps we can take to nurture our faith and remove our fears, starting with this simple principle: feed your faith; starve your fears. And this is how we do it: rather than watching and reading the news day and night, thereby filling our hearts and minds with fearful projections and bad reports, we fill our hearts and minds with God's Word. We read the Word. We speak the Word. We memorize the Word. We sing the Word. We keep the Word before us day and night. We repeat it and recite it. And little by little our souls are washed, our minds are renewed, and our fears are replaced by faith—rock-solid, Bible-based faith.

Notice the common theme of these verses:

> Keep this Book of the Law always on your lips; meditate on it day and night, so that you may be careful to do everything written in it. Then you will be prosperous and successful.
>
> —JOSHUA 1:8

> Blessed is the one who does not walk in step with the wicked or stand in the way that sinners take or sit in the company of mockers, but whose delight is in the law of the LORD, and who meditates on his law day and night. That person is like a tree planted by streams

of water, which yields its fruit in season and whose leaf does not wither—whatever they do prospers.

—PSALM 1:1–3

The person who is blessed, the person who thrives, is the person who meditates on God's Word day and night. (The Hebrew word for *meditate* does not speak of the Eastern kind of meditation, in which you empty your mind, but rather of muttering, hence constantly repeating and reciting.) Jesus gives us a similar promise: "If you remain in me," He says, "and my words remain in you, ask whatever you wish, and it will be done for you" (John 15:7). When we are in Him and His words are in us, our prayers will be in harmony with the will of God and He will answer those prayers.

Proverbs 4 also talks about the importance of keeping God's words stored up in our hearts, never letting them out of our sight: "My son, pay attention to what I say; turn your ear to my words. Do not let them out of your sight, keep them within your heart; for they are life to those who find them and health to one's whole body" (Prov. 4:20–22). Yes, these words literally bring life and health.

And notice what happens when we fill our hearts and minds with the truth of the gospel: "Let the message of Christ dwell among you richly as you teach and admonish one another with all wisdom through psalms, hymns, and songs from the Spirit, singing to God with gratitude in your hearts" (Col. 3:16). There will be joy and gratitude rather than fear and grumbling, and we will minister grace, not grief, to others.

Now, contrast this with reading dire, terrifying news headlines day and night or listening to disturbing newscasts 24/7. What would your frame of mind be? "Things are really bad, and they're only going to get worse! More and more people are getting sick and dying, and the end is not in sight! The stock markets have not looked this bad since the Great Depression!"

This is a series of headlines from the widely read Drudge Report website for March 13, 23, and 24, 2020:[3]

- USA Has 100+ Deaths in Day...

- Testing Blunders Crippled US Response as Coronavirus Spread...

- Biden Slams Trump 'Failure'

- Fear and Foreboding in New York

- California Needs 50,000 More Hospital Beds

- City Dwellers Fleeing to Deserts and Mountains

- Florida Spring Breakers Begin Testing Positive

- Louisiana Has Fastest Growing Cases in World

- Governors Clamp Down Even as President Considers Easing Virus Rules

- Tensions Grow in White House

- Jobless Rate May Soar to 30%

- Commercial Mortgages on Brink of Collapse

- Virus Reveals Financial Irresponsibility of Americans

- Police Tread Lightly as Pandemic Spreads

- I'm 26. It Sent Me to Hospital

- Surgeon General: This Week It's Going to Get Bad

- WHO Warns: 'Accelerating'

- SICK MAP

Headlines like these produce fear and anxiety. They unsettle us and make us feel vulnerable and insecure. They do not build faith or instill hope. Quite the contrary. They produce a feeling of dread. Now, contrast the feeling you get after focusing on the bad news with the feeling you get when focusing on the good news. Take a deep breath, and then read these words slowly and out loud as rendered in the NLT:

> The LORD is my shepherd; I have all that I need. He lets me rest in green meadows; he leads me beside peaceful streams. He renews my strength. He guides me along right paths, bringing honor to his name. Even when I walk through the darkest valley, I will not be afraid, for you are close beside me. Your rod and your staff protect and comfort me. You prepare a feast for me in the presence of my enemies. You honor me by anointing my head with oil. My cup overflows with blessings. Surely your goodness and unfailing love will pursue me all the days of my life, and I will live in the house of the LORD forever.
>
> —PSALM 23

What wonderful, life-giving words—and every one of them is true. Praise God! If you will feast on words like this, which are found throughout the Scriptures, your state of mind will change greatly.

This doesn't mean that you ignore the news or stick your head in the sand. But it does mean that you put your *focus* on what our Father has to say, not what people have to say. And let's remember that there was a time when we did not have 24/7 newscasts, when you would get a newspaper once in a day and perhaps see a news show once at night. That was it. The constant, incessant bombardment of bad news, often sensationalized for ratings, is something new, and it is very unhealthy.

Put on some worship music, and turn off the TV. Listen to a reading of Scripture rather than surf the net. You'll be amazed to see how your attitude changes. And spend some time sharing all your concerns with the Lord, naming them one by one and committing them to His care, with thanksgiving and praise. As Peter urged, "Cast all your anxiety on him because he cares for you" (1 Pet. 5:7). Or, in the words of Paul,

> Do not be anxious about anything, but in every situation, by prayer and petition, with thanksgiving, present your requests to God. And the peace of God, which transcends all understanding, will guard your hearts and your minds in Christ Jesus. Finally, brothers and sisters, whatever is true, whatever is noble, whatever is right, whatever is pure, whatever is lovely, whatever is admirable—if anything is excellent or praiseworthy—think about such things.
>
> —PHILIPPIANS 4:6–8

Cast your burdens on the Lord (Ps. 55:22), worship Him with thanksgiving, and think on the good. Your heart will find rest as you do.

Related to this is the principle of keeping our eyes on Jesus rather than on negative circumstances. Again, this does not mean that we ignore or deny the circumstances. Instead, it means that *in the midst of those difficult circumstances* we keep our eyes fixed on Jesus.

Do you recall what happened when the disciples were at sea in a storm—yes, another storm!—and Jesus came walking on the water toward them? They were terrified to see Him, not recognizing who it was, but once He identified Himself, Peter cried out, "Lord, if it's you, tell me to come to you on the water" (Matt. 14:28).

Now, this was certainly an odd thing to say—why in the world would you ask Jesus to prove His identity by inviting you to get out of the boat? What if it was *not* Jesus? And why not simply invite Him to come into the boat? But it was in fact the Lord, and He said to Peter, "Come" (v. 29).

Matthew records what happened next: "Then Peter got down out of the boat, walked on the water and came toward Jesus. But when he saw the wind, he was afraid and, beginning to sink, cried out, 'Lord, save me!' Immediately Jesus reached out his hand and caught him. 'You of little faith,' he said, 'why did you doubt?'" (Matt. 14:29–31).

So Peter was actually walking on the water, perhaps the only other person in world history to do this, other than the Lord Himself. Peter was doing the "impossible." Peter was walking on the waves! But when he took his eyes off Jesus and saw the wind and the waves, he started to sink. Thankfully Jesus was right there to catch him, which is just like our Lord. But He also had a word of rebuke for him: "Why did you doubt?" (v. 31).

The lesson for us is clear. Keep your eyes on Jesus, not the wind and the waves. Speak out His name when you get a bad report. Praise Him for His goodness when sickness draws near. *Jesus, Jesus, Jesus.* There is something wonderful about that name because there is something wonderful about our Savior. Keep your eyes on Him.

Something else that will help build your faith is filling your heart with God-glorifying testimonies and answers to prayer. If you have kept a prayer journal over the years, you will probably see that many times before, things looked dark, and all you could do was cry out to the Lord for mercy. Reminding yourself of His faithfulness and of these concrete answers to prayer will also alleviate your fears. He can be trusted! Reading and listening to and watching the testimonies of others will also encourage your faith.

It's also true that sometimes there are triggers for our fears, meaning that something that happens today triggers a deep fear from our past. For example, let's say that when you were a little child, your grandfather was killed in a tornado, leaving a deep wound and scar in your heart. As a result, today when you hear about a tornado in another part of the country, you are immediately gripped with an irrational, paralyzing fear, as if someone in your family, hundreds of miles from the tornado, could die.

This is an obvious example, but many times there is a more hidden root to our fears, one that our conscious minds don't grasp. If you have deep, recurring fears, perhaps triggered now by the current crisis, ask the Lord to help you get to the root of those fears, adding His healing grace to your heart.

To my absolute shock, some years ago I started getting panic attacks while flying, something that was utterly bizarre to me. (I love flying, and I'm not a fearful person.) What do you do when you have a panic attack at thirty thousand feet in the air, desperately wanting to get off the plane? Yes, this was a miserable thing to live through, seeing that I spend so much of my time in the air, and it was important for me to understand what was triggering these attacks.

Thankfully some friends with a strong background in counseling and prophetic ministry prayed with me over the phone, and the Spirit helped me understand the root of those fears, bringing healing as well. By God's grace, those attacks are gone. You too can be set free, perhaps with the help of wise and anointed counselors.

Finally, there can be a demonic element to our fears, a tormenting element, a harassing element. I spoke about this in my book *Jezebel's War With America*, explaining how Jezebel in the Bible intimidated even the prophets with fear.[4] She was demonically empowered.

When it's clear that you are being harassed and tormented by the enemy, that's when you should give yourself to prayer, fasting, and taking hold of your spiritual authority in Jesus. Or if you seem too beaten down and oppressed to do that, ask for your leaders to pray over you, breaking this devilish stronghold. In the end fear is empowered by lies. Truth will chase it away. In Jesus' name, be free!

Having laid out these practical guidelines, let's step back and ask a bigger question: Is this the end of the world? Have we entered the last seconds of the last days? Is this virus an end-time plague?

Chapter Three

THIS IS NOT THE END
OF THE WORLD

OES THE BOOK of Revelation predict the
coronavirus? Is it one of the prophesied
end-time plagues? If so, does that mean
that this is just a harbinger of much worse things to
come, just the first of many devastating, consecu-
tive plagues?

On March 26 an article in the *Jerusalem Post*
reported that:

> Devout Christians have taken to social
> media in light of the coronavirus outbreak
> to show the eerie similarities between cur-
> rent events and the prophecy of the end of

the world presented in the New Testament in the Book of Revelation.

The book describes a series of catastrophic events which will ravage the world, some perpetrated by the titular Four Horsemen of the Apocalypse. Though the roles of these riders have multiple interpretations, they are often recognized as: War, Plague, Famine and Death.[1]

Could it be that we are entering apocalyptic times and the plagues and judgments of Revelation are unfolding in front of our eyes? Or is this just the latest wave of Christian sensationalism?

There is no denying the seriousness of the virus. Already on February 28 Bill Gates noted in the *New England Journal of Medicine* that "in the past week, Covid-19 has started behaving a lot like the once-in-a-century pathogen we've been worried about." And, he explained, even at this early stage "Covid-19 has already caused 10 times as many cases as SARS [severe acute respiratory syndrome] in a quarter of the time."[2]

Evangelical commentator Michael Snyder included the coronavirus in his "list of 10 plagues that are hitting our planet simultaneously." The "plagues" are 1) armies of locusts, 2) extremely bizarre weather patterns, 3) unprecedented flooding, 4) major earthquakes, 5) unusual volcanic eruptions,

6) the coronavirus, 7) the African swine fever, 8) the H1N1 swine flu, 9) the H5N1 bird flu, and 10) the H5N8 bird flu.[3]

Does that suggest, then, that COVID-19 is one of the end-time judgments described in Revelation? Dr. Al Mohler noted that,

> We are also reminded of Revelation 6:7–8 in which we read, "When he opened the fourth seal, I heard the voice of the fourth living creature saying, 'Come and see.' So I looked and behold a pale horse, and the name of him who sat on it was Death and Hades followed with him." That fourth horseman has often been associated with plague, with illness, with a violent death by means of this kind of disease, which we now identify primarily with deadly viruses spreading across the human population.[4]

But neither Mohler nor Snyder are suggesting that the virus is one of the final plagues of Revelation. And Gates is certainly not thinking in these terms. To the contrary, the fact that Gates can describe COVID-19 as a "once-in-a-century pathogen" indicates that it is hardly an apocalyptic plague, no matter how deadly it may be.

This is underscored in an article written by Robert Bartholomew in *Psychology Today* titled "The Chinese Coronavirus Is Not the Zombie

Apocalypse." He wrote, "I am not downplaying the seriousness of the new Coronavirus that has been spreading around the world. People are dying and every death is a tragedy. But it is not the end of civilization as we know it—contrary to some media outlets, which risk causing undue alarm and panic."[5] In stark contrast, if the Book of Revelation does indeed describe a series of terrifying end-time plagues, those plagues *will* mark the end of civilization as we know it, along with the ushering in of a glorious new age.

Again, I'm not minimizing the seriousness of the virus. In the words of Israeli Prime Minister Benjamin Netanyahu, "We may be in the midst of not just the worst crisis in a century, but the worst since the Middle Ages." That is saying a lot. As Netanyahu said, "This isn't spin."[6] And certainly "every death is a tragedy." But it was not the end of the world during the Middle Ages either when Europe was ravaged by plague. And it is not the end of the world today. Let's respond wisely rather than react rashly.

To offer my personal perspective, I wrote part of this chapter when returning home from Australia via Hong Kong, where the vast majority of people at the airport were wearing masks, as was the entire crew during the whole flight. And before I passed through airport security in Hong Kong, a wand was held near my forehead to check for a fever. This was done for every single passenger. So again, I recognize the seriousness of this virus. But we minimize the intensity of end-time biblical prophecy by imagining this deadly virus to be an apocalyptic plague.

To be sure, there are many biblical scholars who do not interpret Revelation in this way at all. In their minds many of the events of the book already took place, described in the highly graphic language called "apocalyptic." Others would argue that most of the events are yet future, but they are cloaked in symbolism and should not be taken literally. My own understanding is that there *will* be massive upheaval before the end of the world, in the midst of which there will also be a mighty spiritual outpouring.

But either way, what is clear to me is that we should not view the coronavirus as a prophesied end-time plague. Instead, we should view it in the same way we have viewed many other epidemics and pandemics in world history. They are tragic reminders of the broken state of our world and of the frailty of our race. They are times through which the Spirit speaks and acts, calling us to wake up, to consider our ways, and to repent. And while doing all we can to prevent and combat the spread of COVID-19, we should pray for the mercy of God. The final shaking will be far more intense than this. (I'll come back to this theme in chapter 11.)

But there's another major reason that I do not

believe we have reached the end of the age or that Jesus will be here any second. That's because the biblical judgments are connected with clear words of warning. "Judgment is coming! Repent! Don't let sin destroy you! Turn to God for mercy!" I did not hear such warnings in the months leading up to COVID-19.

Of course, Christian leaders have been sounding *general warnings* like this for decades (or really for centuries), as did biblical prophets in the centuries before them. But I personally believe that as we approach the end of the age, the warnings will become much clearer, calling for specific change in light of specific prophecies, as opposed to a virus just popping up out of the blue.

Really now, where were the *specific* prophetic warnings telling the world that a terrible plague was coming unless we repented? That a pandemic was on the way unless we changed our ways? That a deadly virus would spread like wildfire unless we turned back to the Lord?

I strongly believe in prophetic ministry today, and I believe prophets are called to warn as well as to comfort and equip. Yet among all the prophetic voices around the world today, few, if any, gave a clear warning of what was coming. That alone tells me that this is not an end-time plague.

The first verse of the Book of Amos says, "The words of Amos, one of the shepherds of Tekoa—the vision he saw concerning Israel two years before the earthquake, when Uzziah was king of Judah and Jeroboam son of Jehoash was king of Israel" (Amos 1:1). The prophet brought words of judgment and warning to the nation, and two years later "the earthquake" came.

God was getting His people's attention! Because they didn't repent, refusing to listen to the voices of Amos and the many other prophets, severe judgment followed, including dispersion and exile. But the people had been forewarned.

As stated in 2 Kings 17,

> The LORD warned Israel and Judah through all his prophets and seers: "Turn from your evil ways. Observe my commands and decrees, in accordance with the entire Law that I commanded your ancestors to obey and that I delivered to you through my servants the prophets." But they would not listen and were as stiff-necked as their ancestors, who did not trust in the LORD their God.
>
> —2 KINGS 17:13–14

The same thing happened about 150 years later to the southern kingdom of Judah. They too scorned the words of the Lord:

The LORD, the God of their ancestors, sent
word to them through his messengers again
and again, because he had pity on his people
and on his dwelling place. But they mocked
God's messengers, despised his words and
scoffed at his prophets until the wrath of
the LORD was aroused against his people
and there was no remedy.
                        —2 CHRONICLES 36:15–16

The same thing happened before Jerusalem was
destroyed in AD 70. Jesus Himself warned His
people with tears. (See Luke 19:41–44.) He left no
doubt in the hearts and minds of His hearers. (For
other, related warnings, see Matthew 21.)

Again, I recognize that many pastors and preachers
and prophets have been warning America for years
that judgment was coming. But most of the warnings have been generic as opposed to specific. And
the warnings have certainly not been delivered to
the entire world all at the same time and all about a
coming pandemic if we failed to repent. That would
get our attention. That would be something specific
and dramatic. That would enable us to say to a sinning world, "We told you this was coming, so turn
to the Lord now and ask for mercy before it's too
late!"

With all my heart I believe that when we approach
the final days of planet Earth, meaning that we have

just a few years left before the end, the warnings
will be crystal clear and the judgments, even clearer.
God will speak through prophetic voices, and God
will speak through severe judgments. Yet today we
can't even agree on the origins of the virus. Did
God send it? Did the devil send it? Was it manufactured in a lab? Is it a natural phenomenon?

I do believe that whenever we experience something of this magnitude, we should humble ourselves and pray. We are reminded of our frailty,
of our need for God, of our sin. And it is always
proper to get low, search our hearts, and turn to the
Lord in times of difficulty and pain. In that sense,
as God's people we can always live by 2 Chronicles
7, where God says,

> When I shut up the heavens so that there is
> no rain, or command locusts to devour the
> land or send a plague among my people, if
> my people, who are called by my name, will
> humble themselves and pray and seek my
> face and turn from their wicked ways, then
> I will hear from heaven, and I will forgive
> their sin and will heal their land.
> —2 CHRONICLES 7:13–14

But as children of the Lord we can do this at any
time, in any age, in any country, in any situation.
That is quite different from an end-time, apocalyptic

plague, one of many that will shake the earth at the end of the age. We are certainly not there yet.

Could this be "the beginning of sorrows" (as rendered in the KJV), spoken of by Jesus in Matthew 24:8? He was on the Mount of Olives with His disciples, and as they talked about the beauty and majesty of the temple, He told them that not one stone would be left upon another. In response they said, "Tell us, when will this happen, and what will be the sign of your coming and of the end of the age?" (v. 3). Jesus answered:

> Watch out that no one deceives you. For many will come in my name, claiming, "I am the Messiah," and will deceive many. You will hear of wars and rumors of wars, but see to it that you are not alarmed. Such things must happen, but the end is still to come. Nation will rise against nation, and kingdom against kingdom. There will be famines and earthquakes in various places. All these are the beginning of birth pains.
> —MATTHEW 24:4–8

Is it possible we are in this season now, "the beginning of birth pains"? Scholars debate which parts of Matthew refer to the destruction of the Second Temple, which took place in the year AD 70, and which parts refer to the second coming of Jesus at the end of the age. But let's say for a moment that these verses apply directly to our day today. *Even if that were true*, Jesus is quite explicit: "the end is still to come." Or, as translated in the KJV and other versions, "all these things must come to pass, but the end is not yet." So we *could* be in "the beginning of sorrows," but still the end is not yet.

It is certainly understandable that during times of great upheaval we can think that we are living in the very end of the age: "Everything is falling apart! This is it! We're going downhill from here. It's all over!" But we've been here before, be it with plague or with natural disaster or with war, and we're still here today. The end is not yet.

C. S. Lewis addressed this mentality in 1948 in the aftermath of World War II and the advent of the atomic bomb, and the Gospel Coalition website drew attention to the relevance of his words as we faced today's deadly disease. He wrote:

> In one way we think a great deal too much of the atomic bomb. "How are we to live in an atomic age?" I am tempted to reply: "Why, as you would have lived in the sixteenth century when the plague visited London almost every year, or as you would have lived in a Viking age when raiders from Scandinavia might land and cut your throat any night; or indeed, as you are already living in an age of cancer, an age of syphilis, an age of paralysis, an age of air raids,

an age of railway accidents, an age of motor accidents."

In other words, do not let us begin by exaggerating the novelty of our situation. Believe me, dear sir or madam, you and all whom you love were already sentenced to death before the atomic bomb was invented: and quite a high percentage of us were going to die in unpleasant ways. We had, indeed, one very great advantage over our ancestors—anesthetics; but we have that still. It is perfectly ridiculous to go about whimpering and drawing long faces because the scientists have added one more chance of painful and premature death to a world which already bristled with such chances and in which death itself was not a chance at all, but a certainty.

This is the first point to be made: and the first action to be taken is to pull ourselves together. If we are all going to be destroyed by an atomic bomb, let that bomb when it comes find us doing sensible and human things—praying, working, teaching, reading, listening to music, bathing the children, playing tennis, chatting to our friends over a pint and a game of darts—not huddled together like frightened sheep and thinking about bombs. They may break our bodies (a microbe can do that) but they need not dominate our minds.[7]

Yes, we must not be guilty of "exaggerating the novelty of our situation," and we must "pull ourselves together." The world has been messed up since Adam and Eve fell, and what's happening today, as tragic and deadly as it is, is not a final plague signaling the end of the world. Let us be concerned and sober, but let us not become hysterical.

Without a doubt, we have seen how everything can turn on a dime and how the world as we know it can change overnight. This gives us a foretaste of what could happen in the future and how an antichrist-type figure could ascend to world leadership in a flash. A massive pandemic. A global famine. An international economic collapse. In a moment the world could change and freedoms could entirely vanish.

But I repeat, we have not arrived there yet, and we will do well to remain confident and calm. As Jesus said in Matthew 6 (in the context of worry and anxiety about the future), "seek first his kingdom and his righteousness, and all these things will be given to you as well. Therefore do not worry about tomorrow, for tomorrow will worry about itself. Each day has enough trouble of its own" (Matt. 6:33–34).

Let's work on solving today's very real troubles

rather than worry about the impending end of the age. And when tomorrow comes, let's do the same thing again, always remembering that Jesus truly is Lord. In Him you can be at peace.

Chapter Four

A LITTLE WISDOM
GOES A LONG WAY

A s God's children, we want to be people of
faith. To be bold and unafraid. To obey the
Lord's voice instantly, without hesitation. To
get out of the boat and walk on the water at His
command. We don't want to be wavering back and
forth, in faith one minute and out of faith the next.
That is not the way God's people should live. As
Jacob (James) wrote,

> If any of you lacks wisdom, you should ask
> God, who gives generously to all without
> finding fault, and it will be given to you.
> But when you ask, you must believe and
> not doubt, because the one who doubts is

like a wave of the sea, blown and tossed by
the wind. That person should not expect
to receive anything from the Lord. Such a
person is double-minded and unstable in all
they do.

—JAMES 1:5–8

But notice carefully that Jacob presupposes that
wisdom is also a gift from God. And during times of
crisis and trial we are encouraged to ask the Lord for
wisdom, which we then obtain by faith. Put another
way, faith and wisdom work together as two sides of
the same coin, and one is not in opposition to the
other. Yet some believers struggle when it comes to
finding a balance between wisdom and faith.

For example, wisdom might tell us not to make a
particular financial investment since it is very risky.
But faith might tell us to go out on a limb and God
will bless it. Which is the right course to take, the
course of wisdom or the course of faith?

When it comes to dealing with a virus, do we
put aside all concern and lay hands on every sick
person we find, not worrying about getting infected
ourselves? Do we ignore government guidelines
because they are based on fear rather than faith?
One of my younger colleagues, a godly man who
often prays for the sick, took exception to a video
I produced explaining why we should comply with
governmental guidelines about public gatherings.[1]

He wrote to me privately, saying he was "a little shocked" with my lack of emphasis on praying for healing, feeling that I mentioned it only "in an almost mocking way." (He was referring to my statement that if you had so much faith for healing, then you could stay in your prayer closet and pray until the pandemic stopped.) He felt my video was based in fear more than faith, and he claimed that my "pretense literally disobeys" a host of New Testament scriptures, which he then listed:

> Jesus summoned His twelve disciples and gave them authority over unclean spirits, to cast them out, and to heal every kind of disease and every kind of sickness....Heal the sick, raise the dead, cleanse the lepers, cast out demons. Freely you received, freely give.
> —MATTHEW 10:1, 8, NASB

> And He called the twelve together, and gave them power and authority over all the demons and to heal diseases. And He sent them out to proclaim the kingdom of God and to perform healing....Departing, they began going throughout the villages, preaching the gospel and healing everywhere.
> —LUKE 9:1–2, 6, NASB

Whatever city you enter and they receive
you, eat what is set before you; and heal
those in it who are sick, and say to them,
"The kingdom of God has come near to you."
—LUKE 10:8–9, NASB

Is anyone among you suffering? Then he
must pray. Is anyone cheerful? He is to sing
praises. Is anyone among you sick? Then he
must call for the elders of the church and
they are to pray over him, anointing him
with oil in the name of the Lord; and the
prayer offered in faith will restore the one
who is sick, and the Lord will raise him up,
and if he has committed sins, they will be
forgiven him.
—JAMES 5:13–15, NASB

He then asked me if Jesus did not go against
the governing authorities of His day by healing on
the Sabbath, faulting me for not mentioning that
in my video. (For the question of obeying governmental authorities, see chapter 5.) He wondered if
Jesus would be sheltering in a room today rather
than going out touching lepers, and he felt that if
others had seen God move and heal the way he had,
their perspective and approach would be different.
Isn't this how we love others? he asked. Isn't this
how Jesus loved people, going to where they were,

touching them and healing them? Isn't that what we should be doing?

How do we respond to important questions such as these? Putting aside the wrong personal judgments he made in his email, what about the valid issues he raised? Don't we obey God rather than man? Don't we put aside fear when we pray for the sick, not worrying about catching an infectious disease? After all, isn't the power of the Spirit greater than the power of sickness?

Let me answer these questions with a question. When your little girl has chicken pox, do you bring her to children's church on Sunday and say, "I have faith that none of the other children will be affected," or do you keep her home?

You might answer, "If that was my daughter, I would have faith that none of the other children would get sick. That's how strong my faith is."

I would reply, "I beg to differ, since your faith was not strong enough to keep the sickness off your child in the first place."

A woman named Becky confirmed this to me on Twitter. I had posted the chicken pox question on my Twitter feed.[2] Becky responded: "When my 5 children were very small we went to church, kids went to Sunday school and yep, someone brought their child with fever & full blown chicken-pox! Within days my kids 9yrs and younger had chicken-pox.

My youngest, 13 mos. got so sick spent 9 days in PICU!"[3]

To be sure, I absolutely believe in praying for the sick and have laid hands on thousands of sick people over the years. And in countries such as India, where you often have long lines of people waiting for prayer, I have laid hands on every single one of them, never wondering if I myself could contract some infectious disease in the process.

At the same time, all of us who pray for the sick know that only some will be healed, whatever the reason might be. We cannot guarantee that every person with cancer will be healed or that every blind eye will open. We can preach the Word. We can share the promises of God. And we can pray for the sick. But we cannot guarantee physical healing to every individual we pray for.

It's the same with our own health. We can take good care of our bodies. We can rely on the promises of God. But very few of us live our entire Christian lives without ever getting sick one single time. Not a cold. Not a headache. Not a sore throat. Even fewer of us can say that our spouses and children never once got sick. That is the world in which we live.

In response to my video that asked whether we should lay hands on someone with COVID-19,[4] Karen Anne wrote:

I have led twelve hospital and nursing home teams in Atlanta. I would pray for a coronavirus victim but masked, gloved, sleeved and only if the Lord gave me the green light. I have kids. Honestly, this is so hypothetical even immediate family won't get into ICU. If we know people with mild cases, pray over the phone or messenger because it would not be worth spreading it. Don't operate in foolishness or presumption.

I think as Christians the number one thing we can do right now is to make sure our neighbors are fed, load up your church pantry, give, make meals or soup. We can be there for our anxiety-ridden unchurched friends, we can remind them God is there when they call and that He loves them. This season is a sober, serious season; we must listen to God's direction and not fall into presumption or foolishness. We have to stop believing hoax theories. Actively pray for direction, answers, and cures.

Also in need of prayer are those with canceled elective surgeries! I have a friend in TX in severe gallbladder pain—surgery canceled. (Her name is Tammy if you are praying!) Reach out to these folks and military families with soldiers stuck in COVID-19 hot zones or NYC.[5]

These are words of wisdom, and they lead to a very big question: If you decide to bring one thousand people together in your building for a church service, contrary to government recommendations, can you guarantee that none of them will contract or spread COVID-19? When we have strong and clear reasons for concern with medical experts giving us life-saving guidelines, do we flaunt them in the name of faith?

If I met someone with this virus, I would lay hands on them for healing, and then, barring an instant supernatural result, I would seek immediate testing for the virus and then quarantine myself—not primarily for my sake but for the sake of others. This is the point I will stress in the next chapter: This is about loving our neighbors. This is about being careful.

Again, many of us wonder, "Aren't these restrictions based on fear? And isn't faith the opposite of fear? We don't run *from* the conflict and the crisis. We run *to* it."

To be sure, during times of plague and pestilence, Christians have often served the sick and dying, even at the loss of their own lives. As recounted by Glen Scrivener, summarizing the research of historian Rodney Stark,

> In AD 260, while Marcus Aurelius was emperor, a plague struck (some have thought

it was smallpox). Over a 15-year period, it killed a quarter to a third of the Roman Empire. Stark estimates that at this time there were 45,000 Christians in existence, just 0.08 percent of the empire. Despite their numbers, their response to this pandemic won admiration and a greater following.

Dionysius, bishop of Alexandria, reported: "Most of our brother Christians showed unbounded love and loyalty, never sparing themselves and thinking only of one another. Heedless of danger, they took charge of the sick, attending to their every need and ministering to them in Christ, and with them departed this life serenely happy; for they were infected by others with the disease, drawing on themselves the sickness of their neighbors and cheerfully accepting their pains. Many, in nursing and curing others, transferred their death to themselves and died in their stead."[6]

That is an extraordinary demonstration of the love of Christ, and I have no doubt that many frontline caregivers today are Christians, willing to sacrifice their well-being for the well-being of others. But note carefully that many of these early Christians *died* while caring for others. They were not all supernaturally protected from plague and pestilence (as John G. Lake was in South Africa during the bubonic plague, and as Psalm 91 describes; also, see chapter 12, and note the sad story about a devout gospel preacher, a godly father and husband, who thought we could live like Lake but then died of COVID-19[7]). They stayed among the sick, even at the risk of their own lives. But they did not then go among the healthy once they were infected and spread the disease to others.

In the same way, if you have a healing ministry and get permission to shut yourself in with people dying of the virus, go for it. That's between you and God and your family. May He use you to heal every sick person in the ward and clear the entire hospital! But don't walk into that hospital, lay hands on one hundred infected people, and then go to a crowded restaurant with your family. To do so is to be irresponsible and presumptuous. (And, as Karen mentioned previously, you would not be allowed to do so.)

You say, "But I have faith that I will not get sick and that I will not infect anyone else."

Then show me your faith with your works. Show me all the people who have been healed of COVID-19 through your prayers. Show me your 100 percent success rate. When I see that, I will trust the power of your faith, with joy.

And if you have so much faith, why not just speak the word and heal all the sick? You don't even need to touch them. Or why not just send prayer cloths to the sick, never coming in direct contact yourself? Can't God move in these ways as well, according to our faith?

Even if I am not concerned about my own health, I run the risk of becoming infected and carrying the virus to someone else. (I ask you again, Have you caught a cold as a believer? Gotten sick in any way? Then how can you be 100 percent sure you won't contract the virus?) And so when hundreds of us gather together for a church service, unless we can guarantee that every person there has sufficient faith *not* to be infected, then our gathering presents a potential health hazard to others at a critical time like this. That's why, as we'll discuss shortly, I do not see restrictions on public gatherings as an infringement on our rights as much as an opportunity to love our neighbors.

And should I mention that the first person in Oklahoma to die of the virus was a Pentecostal pastor? As reported on a local news affiliate on March 19, "A Tulsa pastor with no known underlying health problems is the first person to die from Covid-19 in Oklahoma. 55-year-old, Merle Dry, worked for Metro Pentecostal Church for more than 20 years before his death." According to the church, "Dry was in good health before he died as far as they knew. He was fighting a cold and then contracted the virus on Tuesday, according to the church. He caught pneumonia as a complication from Covid-19 and passed away on Wednesday, March 18."[8]

Obviously only the Lord knows the details of Pastor Dry's life and death. But the point is that believers—including Pentecostal believers, even Pentecostal pastors—can contract the virus and die. That's why we use a commonsense approach when combating a pandemic such as this.

A March 29 headline in the *Los Angeles Times* announced, "A choir decided to go ahead with rehearsal. Now dozens of members have COVID-19 and two are dead."[9] That's why I stress that this is also a matter of wisdom, and, as stated previously, the same God who gives faith also gives wisdom. As it is written in Proverbs 22:3, "The prudent see trouble and take cover, but the naive keep going and pay the penalty" (my translation).

What's interesting is that the Hebrew word translated here with "take cover" comes from the same root (*s-t-r*) that is found in Psalm 91:1, speaking of God being our "hiding place." And this is the psalm famous for its promise of protection during plague. (See my Hebrew exposition of the psalm on video,[10] as well as chapter 12.) The same God who provides us with a spiritual "hiding place" also provides us with a natural "hiding place." It is not either-or. It is both-and.

For me personally, fear does not affect my ministry decisions. If I am called by God to go into a dangerous area and preach, I will do it. (For the record, I have done this very thing.) At the same time, the Lord can warn us in advance *not* to go into a certain area precisely because it is dangerous. (This happened to me before traveling to Liberia in 1989 during the civil war there. In prayer I felt the Lord say to me, "Travel at your own risk," meaning, "I'm not promising you protection." I did not make the trip, and my missionary friends there barely escaped with their own lives.)

It is obedience, not fear, that dictates our actions. It is also wisdom that shows us what to do. That's why when we are driving on the highway and there are ice patches forming all over the road, we slow down. That is wisdom, not fear. That's why when there is a hurricane coming, we shutter up the windows. That's also why we lock our doors at night. And why we don't let our five-year-old child wander around the neighborhood. It's called wisdom.

Let us then be people of wisdom, people of compassion, and people of faith, being assured that we will always have plenty of opportunities to exercise our faith. We can exercise our faith today by sharing what we have with others in need (financially and materially). By praying for God to intervene in a pandemic—or any type of crisis—and asking Him to heal the sick and dying. And by not giving place to our fears. Faith and wisdom go hand in hand.

Chapter Five

SHOULD WE SUBMIT TO GOVERNMENT GUIDELINES?

A s AMERICANS WE are fiercely independent. We are not a collectivist society like China, which can mandate the behavior of an entire nation. We are individualists, and we prize our freedoms. And our nation was founded by people seeking freedom from an oppressive government. How then should we respond when our government restricts these freedoms in the name of public safety? Is this an infringement on our constitutional rights? Or is it an opportunity to love our neighbor?

Before answering these questions, we would do

well to consider what is at stake. The *New York Times* painted this grim picture from Italy:

> Hospital morgues there are inundated. Bergamo's mayor, Giorgio Gori, issued an ordinance that closed the local cemetery this week for the first time since World War II, though he guaranteed that its mortuary would still accept coffins. Many of them had been sent to the Church of All Saints in Bergamo, located in the closed cemetery, where scores of waxed wooden coffins form a macabre line for cremations.[1]

And what exactly does this look like?

> "Unfortunately, we don't know where to put them," said Brother Marco Bergamelli, one of the priests at the church. He said that with hundreds dying each day, and with each body taking more than an hour to cremate, there was an awful backlog. "It takes time and the dead are many."[2]

This is what happens when the coronavirus is not checked in time. This is what we could be facing in America.

Here's one more glimpse from the *Times*:

> At around midnight on Wednesday, Renzo Carlo Testa, 85, died from the coronavirus

in a hospital in the northern Italian town of Bergamo. Five days later, his body was still sitting in a coffin, one of scores lined head-to-toe in the church of the local cemetery, which is itself closed to the public.

His wife of 50 years, Franca Stefanelli, would like to give him a proper funeral. But traditional funeral services are illegal throughout Italy now, part of the national restrictions against gatherings and going out that have been put in place to try to stem the spread of Europe's worst outbreak of the coronavirus. In any case, she and her sons could not attend anyway, because they are themselves sick and in quarantine.[3]

Would you like this to happen to your family? Your city? You might answer, "Obviously no one wants something like this to happen, but we cannot let the government overstep its bounds and take away our freedoms. After all, if the government can force us to stay home and stop us from meeting together over this emergency, why not over another emergency? Where does it end?"

One pastor in Iowa, Pastor Cary Gordon, sent me a copy of a long letter (almost three thousand words) that he sent to his congregation explaining why they would be meeting for their Sunday service despite his state government's order not to hold large gatherings. He would use a novel approach, with the people staying in the parking lot in their cars, listening to the sermon on an FM radio signal. And church ushers would go to each vehicle individually to serve Communion. So he was committed to the safety of his congregation. But he felt a public faith statement was also important.

As he wrote with passion and conviction,

> People around the world are frightened because they have not been delivered from the fear of death. They need to see the stamina like that held by the ancient church in the face of darkness. They do not need to only see the face of a feminized, subservient, western church led by hirelings, trembling in the fetal position while the death angel passes across the doors of their homes. So on Sunday, we will take time to pray for our city, state, and nation's salvation and ask God to give us courage and boldness to lead them to Christ by the law of God.[4]

But for Pastor Gordon, this was, above all, a matter of freedom. As he explained,

> We are able to use this opportunity to stand together against the statist abuse of power that is so tempting for those in positions of authority when they are compelled by emergencies and fears to act beyond the

limits placed directly against them by the Constitution of the United States.

"Congress shall make no law respecting an establishment of religion, or prohibiting the free exercise thereof; or abridging the freedom of speech, or of the press; or the right of the people peaceably to assemble..."[5]

Pastor Gordon felt it was absolutely imperative that he and his congregation stand up against dangerous government overreach. He has given me permission to quote him at length. He wrote,

My old fashioned and out-of-date views of our Constitution can get lonely sometimes, but I was so pleased to see that a growing number of people who are legally smarter and more influential than I am joined my chorus this week. The famed Judge Andrew Napolitano published a repudiation of what is going on in an article entitled: "Coronavirus fear lets government assault our freedom in violation of Constitution." I rejoiced when I first saw the title of his article on Fox News.[6] I didn't have to feel quite so lonely anymore. Just this morning I praised God to see the wise Governor of Texas in a televised town-hall meeting on the pending virus threat. He was asked why his executive order closing schools, restaurants, gyms, and limiting people at social gatherings did not include churches. He responded a correct view of constitutional law, stating:

"There was nothing specific in the executive order about churches because there is freedom of religion here in the United States of America."[7] —Governor Gregg Abbott of Texas

Within ten minutes of watching the Texas Governor's excellent handling of the pandemic, my dear friend and former Chief Justice of the Alabama Supreme Court, was quoted in the headlines declaring:

"Economy is destroyed by tyrants who pander fear in the place of faith."[8] —Judge Roy Moore

Then, I was refreshed to see Kentucky Congressman Thomas Massie blast this stinging rebuke about the government errors regarding the Coronavirus:[9]

"When this is over, the greatest harm to society will have been the public's unquestioning acceptance of the unchecked authority of governments to force private behavior and disrupt economies. I fear the actions taken by our government will make FDR's internment of Japanese-Americans look like a 'light touch.'"[10]

These are serious, well-articulated concerns by a sincere Christian leader who is also very serious about not losing our hard-earned American freedoms. And from a medical point of view he questions whether in every case forbidding large gatherings will inhibit the spread of the virus.

But that in turn leads to a simple question for all those who would share Pastor Gordon's convictions: What if we *do* believe the majority of the medical experts? What if we think these are wise guidelines? Then the issue is not so much one of preserving our freedoms. Instead, it is an issue of loving our neighbors. Consequently if the government feels the need to impose reasonable restrictions on the populace in order to save lives, then as much as possible I will comply. I am willing to be restricted so as not to be a potential carrier of the disease to others. This is in harmony with one of the principles of Paul: better to curtail your freedom than to cause someone else to stumble (or, in this case, die).

Of course, Paul was talking about restricting our personal, spiritual freedoms when he addressed this question. (See Romans 14 and 1 Corinthians 8.) He was not speaking of national freedoms and fundamental human liberties. But the same principle applies: love calls us to put limitations on ourselves for the well-being of others.

"But," someone will surely say, "Pastor Gordon is right. We need to look at the bigger picture. This opens the door for the government to do anything. This is just a trial run to see how we will respond. There is nothing random or unplanned about it. The restrictions are part of a larger, national (or even international) plot."

Others, like JJ on the AskDrBrown Facebook page, simply saw this as a major overreaction by our government. He commented:

Huge overreaction and abuse of power with Covid-19. Limited statistics compared to other infectious illness show a massively disproportionate response.

Meanwhile who is calculating the untold risks and even deaths that will occur from job losses, travel bans, nationwide quarantines, food shortages and hoarding, isolation of the elderly, fear campaigns striking terror into many, and on and on.

Yet based on what limited data available, according to all sources from the President down, this is largely a mild illness which the overwhelming majority recover from with only mild cold symptoms, thus majority aren't even tested nor receive medical care who may have had Covid-19. Thus mortality approx. 10-15x less than the seasonal Flu, and nothing remotely resembling the "4%" some have tried to make a case for.

This will go down in history huge overstep

and abuse of Constitutional Rights (recall that we do not serve a President or Institution in America, but as "We the People" they are our Public Servants, and together we are all under the Rule of Constitutional Law). I write this sadly as someone who has largely supported Trump.[11]

These too are valid concerns. How should we respond? The *Christian Post* reported on March 26 that:

> Authorities in countries including Nigeria, Ghana, Uganda and Greece have evacuated church services and arrested pastors in recent days as governments have prohibited large gatherings in an attempt to curb the spread of the novel coronavirus.
>
> As governments across the globe have taken measures to ensure that citizens engage in social distancing so that they don't spread a virus that has already killed at least 21,000 people worldwide as of Thursday, some religious leaders have continued to hold worship services anyway.[12]

Obviously there are Christian leaders around the world who feel that they are conscience-bound to disobey their governments in this matter, whether their reasons are the same as Pastor Gordon's or not. And without a doubt governmental leaders on the local or national level can overstep their bounds. Even the highly respected Liberty Counsel, led by Mat Staver, has raised concerns about government overreach, sending out a press release on March 25, 2020, announcing, "Losing Liberty Is the Long-Term Crisis."

The press release, sent out via email, started by saying, "Governors and mayors have been issuing broad executive orders that are not well vetted and assuming broad powers to shut down businesses with little notice, ordering people to stay home, and imposing fines on violators. Most of the orders operate as if there are no Constitutional protections."[13]

How far then do we let this go? To what degree do we comply as churches? To be perfectly clear, I do not put absolute trust in our government. Not a chance. Nothing close to it. I do not believe in Washington the way I believe in God. (Not within a trillion miles!) And certainly there might be some executive orders that go way too far, on local or national levels, as the Liberty Counsel has noted.

But in terms of the big picture, do we honestly think that President Trump is part of a larger, conspiratorial scheme? That his entire administration is plotting to steal our liberties and subject us to a one-world government (or simply to a federal takeover)? That Trump will be coming for our guns next? Even if the government has overreacted (or is overreacting) out of concern for our health and safety (something that could well be debated for years), should those actions be confused with a frontal assault on our liberties?

I could understand some conservatives being up in arms if George H. W. Bush were our current president, with his frequent references to a "new world order." And I could understand more skepticism from the right if this were happening under President Barack Obama (or more scarily under a President Bernie Sanders).

But let's be realistic. This is happening under Donald Trump. He is nobody's puppet. And he is no friend of the "new world order." It was Germany's Angela Merkel who complained about the damage Trump was doing to this very order.[14] And the Foreign Policy website noted on December 27, 2018, that, "From his earliest days on the campaign trail, U.S. President Donald Trump made clear his disdain for the international organizations that have regulated trade, promoted human rights, and advanced international peace since the end of World War II."[15] That's why I reject the idea that the restrictions being placed on us are part of a larger, nefarious plot.

And it was Trump who said on March 24 (with reference to lifting lots of restrictions), "I would love to aim it right at Easter Sunday so we're open for church services on Easter Sunday, that would be a beautiful thing." And "I think that Easter Sunday and you'll have packed churches all over this country, I think that this will be a beautiful time."[16] Then, on March 26, Trump said, "There is still a long battle ahead, but our efforts are already paying dividends," and he said that "the day will soon arrive" when Americans can resume their "normal economic, social, and religious lives."[17] (At the time of this writing, the president was taking a more cautious position and had amended his prediction that most restrictions would be lifted by Easter, which fell on April 12, 2020, shortly after this book went to press. The point, though, is that President Trump was clearly *for*, not against, our church gatherings.)

It's possible that some leaders want to exploit this crisis to advance their own, controlling agendas. (That would be the likely scenario in China.) But I truly believe that 1) our health experts are doing their best to prevent millions of deaths; 2) our national leaders are doing their best to respond with wisdom; and 3) when it comes to religious liberties, President Trump is our friend rather than our enemy. So unless the ruling authorities order me to disobey God, I will obey the authorities. This is in keeping with Paul's directives in Romans 13:

Let everyone be subject to the governing authorities, for there is no authority except that which God has established. The authorities that exist have been established by God. Consequently, whoever rebels against the authority is rebelling against what God has instituted, and those who do so will bring judgment on themselves. For rulers hold no terror for those who do right, but for those who do wrong. Do you want to be free from fear of the one in authority? Then do what is right and you will be commended. For the one in authority is God's servant for your good. But if you do wrong, be afraid, for rulers do not bear the sword for no reason. They are God's servants, agents of wrath to bring punishment on the wrong-doer. Therefore, it is necessary to submit to the authorities, not only because of possible punishment but also as a matter of conscience. This is also why you pay taxes, for the authorities are God's servants, who give their full time to governing. Give to everyone what you owe them: If you owe taxes, pay taxes; if revenue, then revenue; if respect, then respect; if honor, then honor.

—ROMANS 13:1–7

For those who would say, "But the Word commands us to meet together in Hebrews 10:25, so we must obey God rather than man," I would point out that 1) that is a general directive, exhorting us not to isolate ourselves; 2) we can meet together in smaller gatherings (unless we're in complete shutdown, in which case we can meet in virtual communities online); and 3) this is hardly an attack on our religious freedoms, since it affects strip clubs and bars and movie theaters as much as church gatherings. (See Pastor Gordon's detailed response to questions about Romans 13 on Facebook.[18])

What's interesting is that Paul's next words tie in with our positive calling in Jesus, namely the calling of love. As he wrote,

> Let no debt remain outstanding, except the continuing debt to love one another, for whoever loves others has fulfilled the law. The commandments, "You shall not commit adultery," "You shall not murder," "You shall not steal," "You shall not covet," and whatever other command there may be, are summed up in this one command: "Love your neighbor as yourself."
> —ROMANS 13:8–9

That really says it all, and that's why I do not see these government mandates and guidelines as an infringement on our rights as much as an opportunity to love my neighbor. (And I write this with great respect for those who raise concerns about governmental overreach.)

If and when the government illegitimately seeks to steal our rights, I will join you in standing up and saying, "We must obey God rather than human beings" (Acts 5:29). In fact, over the years, I've done this very thing more than once. This, however, is not such a time. Let us comply based on love and public safety. The sacrifice, overall, is small.

Chapter Six

SEIZE THE MOMENT!

SN'T IT AMAZING how so much of our world changed so dramatically almost overnight? How the new normal suddenly replaced the old normal? How everything is in a state of flux? All this makes us realize how some predicted scenarios that seemed outlandish yesterday don't seem that far-fetched today.

As a kid I remember watching the sci-fi classic *The Day the Earth Stood Still*. As described on Wikipedia, "The film's storyline involves a humanoid alien visitor named Klaatu that comes to Earth, accompanied by a powerful eight-foot-tall robot, Gort, to deliver an important message that will affect the entire human race."[1]

Yes, those were the names, and this was the plot.

Yet "in 1995, the film was selected for preservation in the United States National Film Registry as 'culturally, historically, or aesthetically significant.'"[2] (As I understand it, the 2008 remake did not have the appeal of the original.)

Klaatu has an interplanetary message for Earth, which has developed weapons of mass destruction: "Your choice is simple: join us and live in peace, or pursue your present course and face obliteration. We shall be waiting for your answer." And to underscore this message, he freezes life on planet Earth for a day. Everything comes to a standstill.

Obviously we are not at that point today. (I don't mean with an alien like Klaatu and a robot like Gort; I mean with a total standstill.) Though it may feel as if the world has stopped, it has not: God is still in control. But there is no denying that we are living in unprecedented times, with some nations now discouraging gatherings of more than *two* people, and almost everything else put on hold.

Pastor and evangelist Rodney Howard-Browne was in the news recently, having been arrested in Tampa for defying his county's ban on large gatherings.[3] Whether or not you agree with his controversial decision to continue holding live services at his church, what he wrote recently is striking:

> I talked about what is coming, more than
> ten years. The people in our church are ready

for this. Therefore, nothing of what is happening now is a surprise to me. Every god of America has fallen—sports have fallen, Hollywood has fallen, television shows canceled. Even the god of some mega churches fell, these churches are empty today. I have warned for years that churches will disappear in one night.[4]

He continues,

I hold in my hands the Rockefeller organization document, which was published in 2010. Here is the script that we met today. What is happening now is not an accident; everything was planned. Bill Gates talked about the pandemic four years ago. The document is called "Scenario for Future Technology and International Development," 53 pages. It says here that the result of this scenario will be: "20 percent of the world's population will be infected. People's mobility will be blocked, airports will be closed. Sports events will be canceled, shops closed, theaters closed, churches astounded. A pandemic will produce shortages, including disinfectants and toilet paper. If people refuse the vaccine, they will not be allowed to travel. Political assemblies will be illegal, public protests will be banned. Martial law will be introduced and the new global control system will come into effect. People around the world will be open to sharing their security rights.[5]

And then this:

What is written in the book of Revelation is printed. Globalists lead us to a single government, a single monetary system and the coming of antichrist. And I believe that God raised Trump to suspend it.[6]

Again, whether or not you accept Howard-Browne's larger concerns about the emergence of a one-world government as a result of the pandemic, it's easy to see how something like this could happen. In fact, it's far easier to imagine something like this now than it was back in February of this year. Everything has shifted on a dime. That's why it was no surprise to hear former British Prime Minister Gordon Brown call for a "temporary" world organization—a one-world government of sorts—to fight the current pandemic.[7]

From distant reports of a virus in Wuhan to worldwide upheaval to the point that hundreds of millions of people are fearing for their lives or wondering how they are going to be able to pay their bills. And, to repeat, it happened virtually overnight.

There are several things we can learn from this:

- Nothing is guaranteed in this world.
  Not our next breath. Not the future
  of a nation. Everything can be shaken.
  (See chapter 11.) One day we're
  thinking about what sporting event to
  watch. The next day we're wondering
  about how to feed our families. Or how
  to care for our elderly who are sick.

- God can suddenly get the attention of
  the world. People who never thought of
  praying will start to pray. Carnal concerns will be replaced by eternal issues.
  Life-and-death questions will be asked.

- It does not take much to change the
  international order, with one nation
  rising and another collapsing. The balance of power could shift. Economic
  trends could be reversed.

- We can more easily envision the day
  when the world will have to choose
  between the true Christ and the
  Antichrist. Between God's order and
  the world's order. Between Spirit and
  flesh. Really now, if the coronavirus
  could bring about such rapid change
  around the world, what of a much
  more serious crisis?

Personally I expect life to go "back to normal" in the not-too-distant future. (This is not a prophecy; it is my personal opinion.) But I do believe we need to do some serious reflecting in the midst of the crisis—and learn some serious lessons.

"Normal" life may return for America and the nations. But God's people should give careful thought to their ways, being determined more than ever to live lives that make sense in the light of eternity. Like Klaatu and Gort in the sci-fi classic, the Lord is getting our attention. I say we seize the moment. I say we redeem the time. I say we let Jesus be our example.

Let's look at a famous account in John 9. There we read:

> As [Jesus] went along, he saw a man blind from birth. His disciples asked him, "Rabbi, who sinned, this man or his parents, that he was born blind?"
>
> "Neither this man nor his parents sinned," said Jesus, "but this happened so that the works of God might be displayed in him. As long as it is day, we must do the works of him who sent me. Night is coming, when no one can work. While I am in the world, I am the light of the world."
>
> —JOHN 9:1–5

Do you see what happened here? The Lord never told His disciples *how* this man became blind, other than it was not the result of personal sin. Jesus made clear that the man was not blind because of his parents' sin or his own sin. How then did the man come to be born blind?

Jesus doesn't tell us. He doesn't say, "My Father did it." He doesn't say, "The devil did it." He doesn't say, "This is a purely natural phenomenon." Instead, Jesus says that the man "was born blind so that the acts of God may be revealed through what happens to him" (John 9:3, NET)—meaning through his healing.

Please note that carefully. The Lord didn't say this man was blind to the glory of God but rather that his blindness would be an occasion for the glory of God to be revealed. The man's terrible, difficult, lifelong condition was an opportunity for the Lord to be exalted. That is Jesus' mentality. As He said, "While I am in the world, I am the light of the world" (John 9:5).

The darkness is the divine setup for the light. The sickness is the divine setup for the healing. The current crisis is the divine setup for the church to arise and shine and make a difference. We must seize this moment before it passes (and once the immediate crisis passes, in the aftermath that follows). We must milk it to the full for the glory of God. Does your heart bear witness to my words?

We can seize the moment in our personal lives by taking advantage of changes to our schedule. For me personally, the changes bring financial challenges to our ministry. My team and I will continue to minister and serve as always, putting in many hours a week in the process. And we will do it with joy.

But much of our support comes from average wage earners. If their income dries up, what happens to our support? We also receive substantial support when I travel and speak, as churches receive love offerings for our ministry (as opposed to receiving them for me personally). What happens when meeting after meeting and conference after conference cancels? How do we make up for the loss?

We still have to pay rent. We still have to pay salaries. We still have to pay media bills. We still have to support our missionaries and workers around the globe. How do we do it?

Yes, those are questions I am asking too (but in faith, not in fear), and I mention them here simply to say I understand. I live in this real world too. I understand the pressure.

But that is *not* where my focus is. Instead, I'm focusing on redeeming the time. In fact, it is with some of that redeemed time that I was able to write this book. Less time traveling and speaking means more time in prayer. More time in study. More time writing. More time broadcasting. More time recording. More time reaching out. More time helping others.

These days (or weeks or months) are a godsend to me, something I might not see again for the rest of my life. I have longed for more time alone with the Lord. I have longed for more time to focus on going deeper and being even more fruitful. It has now been dropped in my lap. What will I do with it? What will you do with it?

This can mean more quality family time. (How wonderful!) More time for personal development. More time to catch up on life. More time to get alone and reflect. More time to step back and plan. Let us seize the moment!

Some of you who are parents now have your children at home, and your schedules have become fuller rather than less full. But this too can be a gift from the Lord. Grab hold of these extra hours with your kids. Take advantage of time you would not have had together. Seize the moment!

Let us also use this time to reach out. People are hurting and scared. They are open. They are uncertain. They have questions. And we have answers. We have the hope of eternal life. We have an anchor in the storm. We have faith in a true and living God. We have Jesus and the Spirit and the Word. We have worship and intimacy. We have covenant communities. We have so much to offer right now. We must seize the moment!

Are you shut in your home with little access to the outside world? Then pray for your lost loved ones. Nothing is more powerful than concerted, focused prayer. Or learn to reach out through social media. Perhaps you will develop an effective online ministry in the process.

Are you deprived of your daily distractions, be it sports or entertainment or busywork? Then use the extra time constructively, spending more time to enrich your life and grow as a person. After all, how enriched are you after watching a football game? How much do you grow watching a sitcom? Now is the perfect time to deepen your roots.

Now is also a perfect time to do some serious soul searching. As Leonard Ravenhill often asked, "Are the things you are living for worth Christ dying for?" Does your life make sense in the light of eternity?

As I wrote in my 1990 book *How Saved Are We?*:

> Jonathan Edwards made 70 resolutions by which he patterned his life. Here are just a few of them: "*Resolved*, Never to lose one moment of time, but to improve it in the most profitable way I possibly can.... *Resolved*, To live with all my might while I do live....*Resolved*, Never to do anything

which I should be afraid to do, if it were the last hour of my life." It was Jonathan Edwards who prayed, "Lord, stamp eternity on my eyes." He lived every day in view of forever. "There is nothing like the light of eternity to show what is real and what is not" (Catherine Booth).

Many of us let the circumstances of the moment rule us. We are governed by the pressing needs of the hour. We do not know how to make our schedules submit. We are too busy to accomplish anything of value for God. What matters the least occupies most of our time. What matters the most seldom gets done. Our life is a series of unfulfilled goals. There is plenty of action, but little lasting satisfaction. Our lives are running us instead of us—under God—running our lives.

We must ask ourselves some pointed questions: Are the things we are living for worth Messiah dying for? Are we making the most of every opportunity? Are we living to bring glory to God? Do we realize that we are only passing through this world? "Beware the barrenness of a busy life" (Corrie Ten-Boom).

The few short years we have on this planet could be marked by frustration and futility, or they could be marked by fruitfulness and fulfillment. Who knows just how much could be accomplished through one life yielded up to God? Who knows what God could do through you, if you yielded your all to Him? "Consider what you are missing, both for time and eternity, if you love Jesus with only half a heart" (Basilea Schlink).[8]

Today, with the radical changes that have come to our schedules and our lives, we would do well to slow down, step back, and assess how we live our lives. The rat race is not for us. We are called to something higher and better. And let us look for opportunities to share the gospel and bring comfort and hope. The harvest is exceedingly ripe.

Cultural commentator Bill Muehlenberg wrote,

I am not a prophet, and I am not saying COVID-19 is definitely, specifically the direct judgment of God. It certainly could be. But I do know that God is in control, that God is sovereign. So he most certainly is using this for his purposes.

The only questions we must ask as he shakes the whole world are these: Are we listening? Are we seeking to hear what God is saying? Will we allow God to draw us to himself during these dark times, or will it just be more business as usual?[9]

By God's grace, it must *not* be business as usual. We must seize this moment to the max.

Moses prayed in Psalm 90, "Teach us to number our days, that we may gain a heart of wisdom" (Ps. 90:12). He also prayed, "May the favor of the Lord our God rest on us; establish the work of our hands for us—yes, establish the work of our hands" (Ps. 90:17).

Yes, establish the work of our hands!

Chapter Seven

WHAT IS CHURCH, AND HOW DO WE DO IT?

WE ARE WITNESSING something unprecedented in American history. For weeks on end our church buildings have been empty. Giant sanctuaries that seat thousands of people sit idle. Parking lots normally buzzing with activity are still. What should we be doing at times like this? How should we function as local congregations and as the church at large? Perhaps rather than counting the days until we can gather in large assemblies again, we should learn from the moment. Perhaps we should be asking what the Spirit is saying to the church. (By the time you read these words, our buildings might be open again, but the questions raised here still apply—urgently.)

Lest you misunderstand me, I have nothing against large church buildings or megachurches. To the contrary, I love worshipping with thousands of believers assembled together. I love the dynamic of the anointed music and song. I love the congregational energy when I preach. I love being able to reach so many people at the same time. And I love the way these large congregations can make a massive difference in their communities because of the resources that they have.

Over the years, I have had the privilege of ministering in some of the finest megachurches on the planet, from America to Hungary, from Mexico to Sweden, and from England to South Korea. Many of them are healthy and vibrant, winning the lost, making disciples, standing for righteousness, and supporting world missions. I have also worked closely with house church leaders, and I fully recognize the biblical justification for those assemblies as well as their effectiveness in nurturing the flock and touching the lost.

So my point here is not to bash large gatherings or to fault us for having big buildings. Instead, I'm saying that we need to seize this moment as it relates to the upheaval in our normal church lives. What is the Spirit saying? What important lessons can we learn?

Pastor David Yonggi Cho worked hard to grow a congregation from three people (himself, his wife, and his mother-in-law) to three thousand. He preached hard. He prayed hard. He fasted. He labored. He sacrificed. And he succeeded—at least to a point. Then he had a heart attack, and while lying in bed in the hospital, he received the vision of a cell-based church, with laypeople doing the bulk of the work.

Now, from a biblical perspective, I do not believe in a clergy-laity distinction. We are equally sons and daughters of God, equally branches of the vine, equally priests in God's spiritual temple, equally members of the body. But some are called to be senior leaders, such as pastors and evangelists, and others are not. What Dr. Cho realized was that most of the work was to be done by the body itself, by the "laypeople," not by the senior leaders. And so Yoido Full Gospel Church grew from three thousand people to more than seven hundred thousand people.

Could this time—right now, even if the worst of the 2020 pandemic is behind us—be our corporate "heart attack" moment? Could this be a divinely ordained time to ask ourselves what it means to be the church and how the Lord wants us to function?

Chris Hodges is lead pastor of Church of the Highlands in Birmingham, Alabama, and he explained to Rev. James Robison how his congregation, one of the largest in America, was prepared for the current crisis. He said,

> What we have done, we put into place before this happened. We trained more than 26,000 volunteers and put ourselves in a position financially where we have margins so that when crises like this happen, we can step up. We haven't had to take an offering, we haven't had to train volunteers—they were already ready.
>
> We have a medical clinic downtown that we started and funded. It's under a separate 501(c)(3), but it is our medical clinic called Christ Health Center, and we are using our largest location as a drive-through testing site for coronavirus. Because we had lines of cars for miles, we had to move the location to another place due to the overwhelming response.
>
> As people get within three miles of the campus, they are directed to tune into a short-wave FM radio station. It is playing worship music, playing the Word of God, telling them God loves them, letting them know fear isn't of God and giving them instructions about what the procedures are like when they pull up to the medical professionals.[1]

He also said this, referring to services on Sunday, March 15: "At our church, we've seen people who have never been open to the Lord who are running to God. This past Sunday, during spring break, we would typically have been down 20% to about 40,000 people—and we had 250,000 people watch the service live."[2]

So there's much that can be done in terms of outreach and community service, and there's much that can be exploited in terms of online meetings. We can still be one, even as we are separated by time and space.

Yet there are deeper issues to be learned, issues that have to do with the very meaning of *church*. As I have often stated, the New Testament emphasis is on *being* the church more than on *going* to church. As I wrote in *Revolution in the Church*,

> as surely as a family is not a house, a church is not a building. Perish the thought! Church means people; church means community. It is a fellowship of believers, a congregation of the redeemed, a gathering together of the followers of Jesus. This community, this spiritual family, may meet in a building; but it is not a building, despite the widespread terminology we use.[3]

Yet all too often, as Wolfgang Simson stated in his Fifteen Theses for a New Reformation,

The image of much of contemporary Christianity can be summarized, a bit euphemistically, as holy people coming regularly to a holy place at a holy day at a holy hour to participate in a holy ritual led by a holy man dressed in holy clothes [for] a holy fee.[4]

Now is the perfect time to get out of that mentality. Now is the perfect time to ask, "Lord, what is Your church to be? Who are we, and how are we to function and grow?"

Simson also stated, "Church is a Way of Life, not a series of religious meetings." As he explained,

Before they were called Christians, followers of Christ have been called "The Way." One of the reasons was that they have literally found "the way to live." The nature of Church is not reflected in a constant series of religious meetings led by professional clergy in holy rooms specially reserved to experience Jesus, but in the prophetic way followers of Christ live their everyday life in spiritually extended families as a vivid answer to the questions society faces, at the place where it counts most: in their homes.[5]

I encourage you to look at his Fifteen Theses again. They make for a timely read.

Watchman Nee made similar observations in his classic book *The Normal Christian Life.* He wrote,

> Another thing which is considered of vital importance to the existence of a church is a church building. The thought of a church is so frequently associated with a church building, that the building itself is often referred to as "the church." But in God's Word it is the living believers who are called the church, not the bricks and mortar (see Acts 5:11; Matt. 18:17). According to Scripture it is not even necessary for a church to have a place definitely set apart for fellowship.[6]

He continued:

> The Jews always had their special meeting places, and wherever they went they made a point of building a synagogue in which to worship God. The first apostles were Jews, and the Jewish tendency to build special places of worship was natural to them. Had Christianity required that places be set apart for the specific purpose of worshipping the Lord, the early apostles, with their Jewish background and natural tendencies, would have been ready enough to build them. The amazing thing is that, not only

did they not put up special buildings, but
they seem to have ignored the whole subject intentionally.... The temple of the New
Testament is not a material edifice; it con-
sists of living persons, all believers in the
Lord. Because the New Testament temple
is spiritual, the question of meeting places
for believers, or places of worship, is one of
minor importance.[7]

And what about the substance and style of our
services? What about the things that take place
when we gather together? What about our clergy-
laity distinctions? I also wrote this in *Revolution in
the Church* (and I remind you that I *love* large corporate gatherings and honor senior leaders):

Just look at how our services are structured,
as we come together every week primarily
to hear one man speak. And look at how we
make our leaders the central focus and main
attraction, saying things like, "I go to Pastor
So-and-so's church." And look at the message conveyed by our church services aired
on Christian TV: The leader is the celebrity;
the leader is the anointed one; the leader is
the mediator between man and God. The
average believer cannot possibly compare
with him or her.
Why else would multiplied thousands

of believers (who themselves have direct, immediate access to the Father through the blood of Jesus) seem to have more confidence in the special prayers of the man or woman of God on the TV screen (who will lay his or her hands on hundreds of huge stacks of prayer requests) than in the efficacy of their own prayers lifted before the throne of grace?

Which avails more in the sight of God? You as an individual priest taking your individual petition to the Lord, or a special "holy man" laying his "anointed hands" on a massive pile of prayer requests, included in which is your individual petition? Which prayer is most likely to gain the ear of your Father in heaven? What gets God's attention, personal relationship or powerful anointing? (Remember: The anointing is His anointing. It is His gift in operation.) God is not impressed by the "powerful ministry" of the "man of God," since whatever that man or woman has is a gift from heaven. Relationship is what He values, and humility impresses Him. (See Isaiah 57:15; Micah 6:8.)

We have not yet fully embraced the priestly status of every believer. We have not yet rejected the clergy-laity mentality. We need a revolution in our thinking.[8]

The point is that we are too top-heavy in our structure, too dependent on the anointed and dynamic speaker, too reliant on the super-gifted worship team. It seems that performance is more important than substance and that putting on a show is more important than making disciples. Yet even in these times of upheaval, some of us are still trying to duplicate the big, corporate dynamic—only by livestream to our homes—rather than ask larger structural and philosophical questions.

One of my ministry school grads, himself a house-church planter, wrote this to me:

> People are really coming into correct view of their own vulnerability and mortality. The churches are doing a great job encouraging, comforting, and helping the community.
>
> My only concern is that the livestream phenomenon is encouraging churches to embrace concert Christianity, with live bands and sermons from stages with empty pews, when I thought this may be an opportunity for them to think creatively and embrace more homestyle meetings.
>
> I also feel as if this is a dry run as a birth pang for the end times. And we are in too much of a rush to get back to normalcy rather than learn the lessons of what the end times could look like.

He added,

> I talked to a large-church pastor today and
> he said to me that he was sad that they
> had to go to livestream services because
> his church isn't prepared to only do home
> groups. He said that he was grieving and
> thinking about how he could better prepare
> his church after this.
>
> But I am shocked at the number of pas-
> tors who don't want to do livestream ser-
> vices, but that is all their people know and
> are used to.
>
> We have a need to prepare people for the
> coming times.

We are definitely in a trial run today. How will
we respond?

To say it once more, I love large corporate gatherings, and I have friends who are megachurch pastors. They are some of the finest leaders I know, and
they are deeply committed to fulfilling the Great
Commission. For them quality counts far more
than quantity. In fact, for some, quantity is only
important if it translates to quality. As Pastor Andy
Stanley told me during a radio interview, the only
numerical goal he and his leadership team have
for his church is one hundred thousand people in
home groups, being discipled.[9]

I also love doing livestreams whenever I can,

finding this to be a fantastic way to reach people around the world via internet. What a great tool! These days I'm using it more than ever. I have had a daily live radio broadcast for the last twelve years; as well I have hosted several shows on Christian TV. So I am *not* faulting large gatherings. I am *not* faulting large buildings. I am *not* faulting the use of media, and I am *not* faulting large ministries.

What I *am* saying is that these large gatherings and buildings and ministries and methods can often take our eyes off of what it means to be the church. What it means to be disciples. What it means for each of us to be salt and light. What it means to be sent and commissioned by God—each and every one of us.

In many ways we have become too tame, too domesticated, too much like an audience. It's time we recapture our *roar*. It's time we become dangerous to darkness. It's time each of us gets equipped and engaged.

Around the world for almost two thousand years the church has grown without church buildings and without livestreaming. What would happen today in America if for one year we could not gather in a building and we could not meet via internet? How would we find fellowship? How would we reach our neighborhoods? How would we grow in the Lord? How would we serve the hurting?

Perhaps if we asked these questions today, both

as leaders and individual believers, then, if and when we could regather in buildings and online, our whole mentality would be different. Our whole mentality would be healthier.

Let us learn from this unique season in our history, not only redeeming the time but also redeeming the moment. Jesus, what are You saying to us? What do You want from Your church? Who are we to be? How are we to live?

Acts 8 tells us that when Stephen was martyred, "On that day a great persecution broke out against the church in Jerusalem, and all except the apostles were scattered throughout Judea and Samaria. Godly men buried Stephen and mourned deeply for him. But Saul began to destroy the church. Going from house to house, he dragged off both men and women and put them in prison" (vv. 1–3).

This was really bad news. Persecution is never fun. But, the text continues, "those who had been scattered preached the word wherever they went" (v. 4). The persecution led to the expansion of the kingdom. The gospel message was spread.

That is God's heart for His people in this hour. May the inconveniences and even hardships we encounter lead to the growth of the church and the greater reach of the gospel for the glory of Jesus' name.

Chapter Eight

STEWARDING OUR
HEALTH AND CARING
FOR EVERY LIFE

THINK ABOUT IT for a moment. Countries such
as England banned public gatherings of *more
than two people*. Israel fined people for *walking
more than one hundred meters* outside their homes
without due cause. Cities throughout the world
shut down. Life as we have known it for decades
virtually stopped. Why? Because of a deadly virus,
because we were concerned that multiplied tens of
millions of people could die. That's why we took
such extraordinary measures: life is extraordinarily
precious, and we must do whatever we can do to
save lives.

Yet there is a tragic irony in our heroic efforts to save lives. Every day people die needlessly. Every day people suffer without good reason. Every day lives are cut short—all because we do not take proper care of our bodies. All because we do not guard our health. All because we do not steward our diets. This makes no sense at all.

Think about it. We shut down professional sports. We close our children's schools. We cancel thousands of flights. The government has to come up with trillions of dollars of relief. We do it all to save lives, and it is very good that we do it. Yet to save and preserve our own lives, we're not willing to put down a french fry. Or a cheeseburger. Or a slice of pizza. Or a milkshake. Or a donut. Why?

Dr. Joel Fuhrman, famous for his books including *Eat to Live*, explained that,

> Heart disease is the number one killer in the United States, accounting for more than 40 percent of all deaths. Each year approximately 1.5 million Americans suffer a heart attack or myocardial infarction (MI); more than 400,000 of them die as a result. Most of these deaths occur soon after the onset of symptoms and well before victims are admitted to a hospital. Every single one of those heart attacks is a terrible tragedy, as it could have been avoided.[1]

In our book *Breaking the Stronghold of Food*, my wife, Nancy, drove home the point:

> To reiterate what many medical professionals have said (and clinically proven), diseases such as diabetes, heart disease, and high blood pressure are primarily brought on by overweight, obesity, and unhealthy eating—and our overweight, obesity, and unhealthful eating are entirely under our control. We don't have to succumb to these illnesses if we choose rightly. It's entirely up to us. So do we choose those things that do our bodies good or do we choose what does them harm? It's our choice alone.[2]

And this is the real tragedy: far more people will die every year from preventable diseases than have died in recent pandemics. Millions of lives will be needlessly lost—precious lives, lives that count and matter. We're talking about dads who never got to walk their daughters down the aisle and grandparents who passed away when they were about to enjoy retirement. We're talking about people you know and love, some of whom could still be with us today. Yet because of poor food choices and addictions to unhealthy foods (perhaps all done in ignorance), they are no longer with us. This is a staggering truth.

According to the World Health Organization (WHO),

> Cardiovascular diseases (CVDs) are the number 1 cause of death globally, taking an estimated 17.9 million lives each year. CVDs are a group of disorders of the heart and blood vessels and include coronary heart disease, cerebrovascular disease, rheumatic heart disease and other conditions. Four out of 5 CVD deaths are due to heart attacks and strokes, and one third of these deaths occur prematurely in people under 70 years of age.[3]

If only half of these deaths could have been prevented through healthy eating and living (which is an extremely low estimate), that would mean that every year about nine million Americans die before their time. Yet the last pandemic, the H1N1 swine flu, killed between 151,700 and 575,400 people, according to the Centers for Disease Control and Prevention.[4] Do you see why I'm raising this issue? This is also quite relevant when it comes to COVID-19 (and many other viruses and diseases), since the best defense against sickness and infection is a strong immune system. And the best way to strengthen our immune systems is by long-term healthy eating. As explained by Dr. Fuhrman,

The immune system is the body's defense system against irritants, toxins, infections, and the development of cancer. With an arsenal of "soldiers," such as T-cells, B-cells, antibodies, macrophages, etc., the immune system can detect, attack, and remove potential dangers to optimal health. A nutrient-dense eating style with a variety of immune supporting phytochemicals is required to maintain an effective immune system.[5]

Put another way, healthy eating will help keep you healthy. It really is that simple.

Allow me to bring in a biblical illustration. Naaman was a powerful Syrian general who held a prestigious position in his country. He was also a leper. Yet there was an Israelite slave girl serving Naaman's wife, and she remarked one day, "If only my master would see the prophet who is in Samaria! He would cure him of his leprosy" (2 Kings 5:3). She was speaking of the prophet Elisha.

So with the king's blessing, Naaman went to see Elisha (I'm condensing the story), expecting the prophet to make some grandiose entrance and, with a flamboyant act, pronounce Naaman healed. Instead, Elisha sent his assistant, Gehazi, to Naaman with this message: "Go, wash yourself seven times in the Jordan, and your flesh will be restored and you will be cleansed" (2 Kings 5:10). Naaman was incensed and said, "I thought that he would surely come out to me and stand and call on the name of the LORD his God, wave his hand over the spot and cure me of my leprosy" (v. 11).

This was too easy, too demeaning, too impersonal. He continued, "'Are not Abana and Pharpar, the rivers of Damascus, better than all the waters of Israel? Couldn't I wash in them and be cleansed?' So he turned and went off in a rage" (v. 12).

But the story doesn't end there:

> Naaman's servants went to him and said, "My father, if the prophet had told you to do some great thing, would you not have done it? How much more, then, when he tells you, 'Wash and be cleansed'!" So he went down and dipped himself in the Jordan seven times, as the man of God had told him, and his flesh was restored and became clean like that of a young boy.
>
> —2 KINGS 5:13–14

Now, if you're still wondering why I shared this story here, the reason is simple. We are willing to go to extraordinary measures to save human lives— including our own—but we're not willing to do the simple, everyday things. Or could it be that we are simply ignorant of the importance of healthy eating?

Before international flights were shut down, I flew to Australia and back via a very circuitous route: Charlotte, North Carolina, to New York City to Hong Kong to Sydney to Brisbane, Australia, returning home on a similar route. During this long trip, which was in the early days of the coronavirus concerns, I reflected a lot about my own health, writing a passionate appeal to my fellow ministers. Here's the text of that article from March 8. It applies to every single one of us, not just those of us in vocational ministry.

A Personal Appeal to My Christian Ministry Colleagues: Please Guard Your Health

As a fellow leader in the Body, I understand the constant pressure you are under. I do not want to add to that pressure. I also understand the amount of negative judgment you have to deal with. I am not here to judge or criticize. Instead, as a co-worker in the Lord, I want to make an appeal to you. Please take care of your health. We need you on the front lines.

As many of you know, by God's amazing grace, I made a radical lifestyle change on August 24, 2014, breaking the habit of 59 years of unhealthy eating. Yes, the same person who was a lifelong chocoholic, eating Oreos for breakfast as a boy and who often had pizza every day of the week as an adult, that same person is now a poster boy for healthy eating.

It is an ongoing miracle of grace, as the Lord has helped me to stay disciplined, eating only healthy foods, without exception, regardless of where I'm traveling. Or who I'm with. Or what the occasion is. The benefits are hard to put into words. Without exaggeration, I can say that I'm feeling younger every year that I get older, and my overall health is off the charts.

I'm not just talking about excellent cholesterol and blood pressure levels. I'm talking about not having a single headache in more than 5 ½ years. (I used to have several headaches a week.) I'm talking about no more sleep apnea (which means no more breathing machine to travel with). I'm talking about much more energy and a much stronger immune system. And so much more.

That's why I'm making this appeal to each of you. We need you to be strong and healthy and running your race. We need you vibrant and sharp. We need you full of life. Your family needs you. Your congregations and ministries and organizations need you. And the world needs you too. Will you be a good steward over your body? Will you guard the gift of health?

Of course, there are many things that are out of our hands. There are sicknesses and diseases that are beyond our control. And none of us are exempt from accidents or calamities. Our lives are truly in God's hands, and some of you are demonstrating your spirituality and faith by glorifying Him in the midst of sickness and pain. But there are many things that *are* up to us, and we are called to be good stewards of everything the Lord entrusts to us. Few things are more important than our health.[6]

You might ask, "Why write this article now? I'm glad you're doing well, but it's not like you just celebrated some special anniversary. Why the strong appeal today?" Well, there are two main factors that prompted me to write.

First, I just traveled to Australia and back, with roughly one hundred hours of round-trip travel and only seventy-two hours on the ground to minister. (This was due to some flight cancellations and visa delays, making for some lengthy and convoluted travel routes.) What this meant was that it was roughly fifty hours from leaving my house to arriving at my destination in Brisbane. Then, I had to speak within two hours of my arrival.

I was then home for less than seventy-two busy hours before leaving for Chicago for ministry, then Atlanta, then New York City. (This is not my ideal schedule; it just happened due to some scheduling errors.) Time zones varied by up to sixteen hours. Temperatures varied greatly. The speaking schedule was full. Yet I have been thriving and strong in the midst of it, just days short of my sixty-fifth birthday.

I am quite sure that without my healthy eating regimen, which, again, I attribute wholly to God's mercy and grace, I would be exhausted, sick, or flat on my back. Others notice it too, always asking me about how I eat and live. I give all the glory to the Lord.

Yet so many people suffer from self-inflicted conditions, conditions that would disappear totally with a healthy eating regimen. Yes, many serious illnesses can be totally reversed. And since we are purchased by the Lord and He owns us (including our bodies), shouldn't we make every effort to steward our physical temples? Isn't this part of how we glorify the Lord? Isn't self-control a fruit of the Spirit?

If I sound condescending or condemning, please forgive me. That is the opposite of what I intend. Instead, take this as a divine invitation to vibrant health and living. It is so absolutely worth it. Whatever carnal pleasures you might have to sacrifice by giving up your favorite indulgences will be massively outweighed by the joyful abundance of healthy living.

The second reason I'm covering this subject is

that my travel route took me through Hong Kong, and concerns about the coronavirus were everywhere. A strong immune system is our greatest line of defense against this kind of virus (even the common flu virus), which could literally mean the difference between life and death. At times like this we benefit greatly from a healthy lifestyle.

Again, our lives are in God's hands, and I do not boast about tomorrow. Instead, as a recipient of the Lord's transforming mercy I commend that same mercy to you. May you be blessed with discipline, self-control, and thriving health, running your race so as to win and finish well. I'm cheering you on!

OLD LIVES MATTER

Sadly, for many now is not the ideal time to make a radical diet change. That's because—as I write these words—they are fighting for their lives in a hospital right now, hoping to survive this deadly plague. And many of them are elderly, which leads to one more crucial subject for us to consider today, since we're hearing all the time that almost all the people who are dying from the coronavirus are old.

But what is this supposed to mean? Does it mean that younger people don't need to worry about contracting it? Or does it mean something worse, as in old people really don't matter?

As for the first attitude, namely that younger people need not be concerned about the virus, that is hardly true. As *USA Today* reported on March 19, "It's not just adults 65 and older. Americans of all ages have faced serious health complications amid the new coronavirus outbreak, a federal health report says.

"New data from the Centers for Disease Control and Prevention show that among the roughly 12% of COVID-19 cases in the U.S. known to need hospitalizations, about 1 in 5 were among people ages 20 to 44."[7]

Even college-age students returning from spring break have tested positive.[8] And while their risk of serious illness or death is much lower than among the elderly, they are not immune.

As for the elderly, they are truly suffering. In Italy the average age of those dying from COVID-19 is over seventy-nine (and almost all had preexisting conditions).[9] And things are now so dire that an Israeli doctor working in northern Italy explained that "patients over 60 tend to receive less treatment with anesthesia and artificial respiratory machines."[10] Better to treat those who have more hope of survival.

In England the first two members of London's ultra-orthodox Jewish community who died of the virus were 97 and 85.[11] Yes, it is the elderly in particular who are perishing.

But that doesn't mean that old lives do not matter. To the contrary, from a biblical mentality it is the elders who should be especially esteemed and honored. They are the ones who have worked a lifetime and accumulated decades of wisdom and experience. They are the ones who have seen fads come and go. They are the ones who have raised families and led businesses. They are the ones who have sown many years and should be allowed to reap. The more fragile they become, the more care and love they should receive.

But that's not how our modern American society thinks. Life is for the young. For the beautiful. For the athletic. For the virile. Life is for those with chiseled bodies, not wrinkles.

The annual Old-Timers' baseball game may be nostalgic, but it's really sad to see how these great stars have aged. The sentimental movie about a couple grown old may be a real tearjerker, but we'd much rather see a superhero in action. Life is for the young!

Of course, young people *should* enjoy life. There are some things you can do when you're young that you can't (or wouldn't) do when you're old. There are things you can learn. Sports you can enjoy. Hobbies you can tackle.

Life can be wonderful for young people, and it should be enjoyed as much as possible. Let us all live life to the full. But there's a reason that the president has to be at least thirty-five years old. Would you want a twenty-year-old commander in chief?

There's a reason that Alfred Gruenther became the youngest four-star general at the age of fifty-three.[12] There's a reason that the vast majority of respected scholars and scientists are in their forties and beyond. There's a reason that older people teach younger people in college rather than the reverse. There's a reason that the average age for a Fortune 500 CEO to be hired is fifty-seven[13] and the average age for an NFL head coach is forty-eight.[14]

Good things take time, and wisdom and knowledge are not obtained overnight. That's why it's not surprising that both President Trump and the two leading Democratic candidates are in their late seventies.

I just turned sixty-five myself, which officially makes me a senior citizen. But I feel just as vibrant, just as mentally sharp, just as full of vision and energy as I did in my twenties. Slowing down is not on my mind, and I feel confident that in the Lord I have more to offer today than at any time in my past.

My esteemed colleague James Robison, himself seventy-six, also texted this to me about older Americans:

> The enemy does want to destroy the elders, the 60, 70 and older because they have a wiser, broader perspective and have observed the consequences of our actions. Also, they control over 50% of America's

wealth and can, if led by God, take the gospel of the Kingdom to all nations now!

According to Harvard Research, people 74 and older control 21% of America's wealth—21 trillion dollars. Combine that with those 58 and older, and 75% brings the total controlled to 75 trillion dollars. According to *Forbes* the least moved by biblical truth millennials will inherit 68 trillion dollars by 2030.

He added,

> If this wealth is not directed by the elders with godly wisdom, the money He trusted them to oversee will fund the enemy's destruction of the very freedom the Father freely offers to the just and the unjust. Time to "arise and shine" with His glory all over us!

To that I say amen!

Of course, from a medical standpoint I do understand that countries like Italy have had to make terribly difficult decisions, asking who is more likely to live. And more broadly, I absolutely believe in the potential and gifting and calling of young people. They are world changers too, and it was people like Bill Gates and Steve Jobs and Mark Zuckerberg who, as young men, greatly shaped the world we live in today. (I say that for better or for worse.)

One of my greatest joys is to teach and mentor young people, and there is nothing more important than joining the generations together. All the more, then, do we need to stand with and for the elderly in our midst. For the grandparents and great-grandparents. For the pioneers and builders. For those who still have so much to offer and to give.

And so rather than this pandemic trivializing the importance of older lives, let the reverse be true. Let it remind us every day that old lives really do matter—a lot. And let us cherish our own health—if not for ourselves, then for others and for the Lord. And let us not cut our lives short through foolish and fleshly choices but work *with* our Creator rather than *against* Him. It would be a great outcome from this deadly virus if in the end millions more lives could be saved than lost as we learned the lesson of stewarding our health.

Chapter Nine

THE GOSPEL IS MADE FOR THE HARD TIMES

J EREMIAH THE PROPHET had a very difficult life. He was called by God at a young age—most likely as a teen—yet was forbidden by the Lord to marry or have children. He was rejected. Hated. Beaten. Imprisoned. Mocked. Falsely accused. Abandoned to die. Yet he never altered his message for a period of forty years, proclaiming judgment and destruction if his nation would not repent.

But sometimes things got too intense. The pressure was too great, the sting of rejection too painful, the dire message too overwhelming. And at times like that even Jeremiah broke down, not changing his message but telling the Lord he was done. "I don't need to prophesy any longer!"

This happened in Jeremiah 20, after he had been put in the stocks and then had delivered a message of judgment to the man who locked him up. He wished he had never been born. He tried to suppress the message, but he could not. It was like fire in his bones.

It happened in Jeremiah 15, after he had delivered yet another agonizing word of death and devastation and bereavement. "Woe is me!" he proclaimed. He had really had enough.

And it happened in Jeremiah 12 after his own family had turned on him and close relatives wanted to put him to death. (See Jeremiah 11:18–23.) It was time to make his complaint known to God, and we read it beginning in Jeremiah 12:1. Unfortunately many of our English translations take the sting out of his words, with translations that say something like, "Righteous are You, O LORD, when I plead with You; Yet let me talk with You about Your judgments" (NKJV).

What the Hebrew is really saying is much more confrontational, and to drill the point home, I would translate it like this: "I know that You'll always come out in the right when I lodge a complaint with You; nonetheless, I'm going to bring charges (or, make a judgment) against You." Those are biting words!

Specifically, Jeremiah questions the way the Lord runs His world, saying:

> Why does the way of the wicked prosper? Why do all the faithless live at ease? You have planted them, and they have taken root; they grow and bear fruit. You are always on their lips but far from their hearts. Yet you know me, LORD; you see me and test my thoughts about you. Drag them off like sheep to be butchered! Set them apart for the day of slaughter! How long will the land lie parched and the grass in every field be withered? Because those who live in it are wicked, the animals and birds have perished. Moreover, the people are saying, "He will not see what happens to us."
>
> —JEREMIAH 12:1–4

And how does the Lord reply? How does our gracious heavenly Father treat His hurting, loyal son? He rebukes him! He basically says to him, "Jeremiah, if you're having a hard time making it in your little hometown of Anathoth, how are you going to make it in a big city like Jerusalem? If a little pressure from your family makes you question how I run My world, what are you going to do when things get rough?" Or, to use a traditional (but today politically incorrect) phrase, "Jeremiah, man up!"

The Lord said to him, "If you have raced with

men on foot and they have worn you out, how can you compete with horses? If you stumble in safe country, how will you manage in the thickets by the Jordan?" (Jer. 12:5). And this was just what Jeremiah needed. He was strengthened and continued in his mission. "No more complaining, Lord! I realize this is bigger than me."

To be sure, the Lord also offered him comfort, basically saying in the verses that follow, "Jeremiah, I understand. My own family has turned on Me too, and I must hand them over to judgment." But that was not the first thing God said to him. Instead, He pushed back against the prophet's complaint and jarred him back into reality.

That is exactly what some of us need. We need to be jarred back into reality. We need a divine jolt to our senses. We need a holy wake-up call. (Dare I call it a loving slap in the face?)

For many of us now, things may be bad, and for some of us, things may be very bad, even dire, to the point of overwhelming. *I am not downplaying the pain or the panic or the crisis or the craziness.* Death is death. Upheaval is upheaval. These really are unprecedented times—but then again, they are not so unprecedented after all. Throughout history we have experienced living hell in this world, and throughout history we have survived. What's more, throughout history we have overcome.

Look at Paul's words in Romans 8:28–37, words

that are not just poetic and beautiful. They are also gritty and real. Paul has stated that "we know that in all things God works for the good of those who love him, who have been called according to his purpose," after which he laid out the glorious plan of salvation (Rom. 8:28–31).

This prompted Paul to write, "He who did not spare his own Son, but gave him up for us all—how will he not also, along with him, graciously give us all things?" (Rom. 8:32). God already did the hard part, giving up His Son. The rest is easy!

Paul continues, "Who will bring any charge against those whom God has chosen? It is God who justifies. Who then is the one who condemns? No one. Christ Jesus who died—more than that, who was raised to life—is at the right hand of God and is also interceding for us" (Rom. 8:33–34). What incredible truths!

And then, based on this confidence, he asks, "Who shall separate us from the love of Christ? Shall trouble or hardship or persecution or famine or nakedness or danger or sword?" (Rom. 8:35). Then his dramatic answer: "As it is written: 'For your sake we face death all day long; we are considered as sheep to be slaughtered.' No, in all these things we are more than conquerors through him who loved us" (Rom. 8:36–37).

Do you see what Paul is saying? We *are* being slaughtered like sheep (quoting Ps. 44:11). We *are* experiencing trouble and hardship and persecution and famine and nakedness and danger and sword. We *are* going through terrible times of suffering and hardship and pain, but *none* of it can separate us from Messiah's love. Through Him we are more than conquerors. This makes me want to shout!

Harold J. Chadwick asked:

> Would you suffer persecution, poverty, and prison for Christ? Would you endure cruel tortures that take your mind and body to the very brink of death and beyond? Would you persevere? Would you "hold fast the profession of your faith without wavering?" (Heb. 10:23, KJV) Would you stand boldly without shame and confess Christ as Lord, to your own or to your family's peril? For two thousand years, courageous men and women have been tortured and killed because of their confessions of Jesus Christ as Lord.[1]

Throughout history God's people have experienced hardship of every kind, be it persecution for the faith, or be it the difficulties of life. And throughout history God's grace has carried us through, making His strength perfect in our weakness. There is no shortage of His power and help today.

So to the weak God says, "Be strong in the Lord!" (See Joel 3:10; Ephesians 6:10.) You might be weak and frail, but in Him you are an overcomer. And so the Spirit says to us, "Don't feel sorry for yourself. Don't throw a pity party. Don't identify with your problems. Instead, put on God's armor and be strong in Him. You are more than a conqueror through Jesus!"

Let me stir your heart for a moment with some stories of courage from the first centuries of church history, when believers paid with their blood for their faith. (I assure you that they would not be able to relate to today's soft, me-centered gospel, where "persecution" for us is being unfriended on Facebook.)

As the early church leader Ignatius was on his way to be martyred, he famously wrote, "Now I begin to be a disciple....Let fire and the cross, let the companies of wild beasts, let the breaking of bones and the tearing of limbs, let the grinding of the whole body, and all the malice of the devil, come upon me; be it so, only may I win Christ Jesus!"[2] He joined other pioneer martyrs such as Paul and John and almost all of the original apostles. Leadership in the church came with a price.

Frank Di Pietro offers this account of the martyrs in Palestine and Phoenicia in the centuries that followed:

> After intense floggings they were thrown before man-eating beasts: leopards, bears of

all kinds, wild boars, and bulls goaded with hot irons. The man-eaters...did not touch or even approach those who were God's beloved, but attacked the men who were goading them. The holy champions, though they stood naked and waved their hands to attract the animals, as they were ordered to do, were left untouched. When the beasts did rush them, they were stopped, as if by some divine power, and would retreat... astonishing the spectators...at last after countless assaults by these animals, the martyrs were then all butchered with the sword.[3]

And this account from Egypt:

Thousands of men, women, and children went to their deaths for the sake of our Savior's teachings. Some of them were flayed, racked, ruthlessly whipped, and tortured in ways too terrible to describe and finally given to the flames or drowned in the sea. Others were nailed to a cross, head downward, and kept alive until they died of hunger....Many had their bodies torn to shreds with claw-like potsherds until they expired. Women were tied by one foot and swung high in the air, head downward, by machines, their bodies totally naked....

> Others died fastened to trees: they bent
> down the strongest branches by machines,
> fastened one of the martyr's legs to each,
> and then let the branches fly back to their
> natural positions, instantly tearing apart
> the limbs of their victims. This went on not
> for a few days but for whole years.[4]

And the story continues to this day, with our brothers and sisters around the world suffering great tribulation for their faith. But Jesus promised that we would suffer, saying, "I have told you these things, so that in me you may have peace. In this world you will have trouble. But take heart! I have overcome the world" (John 16:33). Or as Paul and Barnabas said to the believers in Antioch, "We must go through many hardships to enter the kingdom of God" (Acts 14:22). And they spoke these words to *encourage* the believers, not to discourage them.

In India I have washed the feet of a martyr's widow (I had previously laid hands on her husband and commissioned him to preach before he was killed) as well as washed the feet of Indian pastors who have been beaten for their faith yet returned to preach to the people who beat them. Some of them were subsequently martyred for their faith. Yet when we finished washing their feet, rather than leave the meeting depressed, they began to leap for joy and celebrate, counting it a great privilege to suffer for Jesus' sake. (See Matthew 5:10–12.)

Of course, it is one thing to suffer for the gospel; it is another thing to suffer because of a pandemic. But the point I'm making is the same: The gospel is made for hard times. The gospel can carry us through. God's grace is always sufficient, no matter what we endure. That includes losing your children because of a freak accident or losing your grandparents because of a virus. That includes losing your business due to bankruptcy or losing your reputation due to obedience.

Whatever our situation, whatever our generation, whatever our dilemma, whatever our challenge, God will see us through. Through His Son we overcome! And the things that were meant to destroy us can be the very things that make us stronger.

My good friend Scott Nary, himself a powerful evangelist, recently posted this on Facebook:

> My whole life I've been a fighter. I was inspired by my parents. My father was a coal miner, his father was a coal miner and his father's father was a coal miner.
>
> Hardship was our norm and fighting through hardship was expected.
>
> I wasn't handed a silver spoon of entitlement. I had to bust my butt with hard work and tenacity that I picked up by watching the West Virginia coal miners' work ethic.

Today I am thankful for my upbringing. I wasn't given an easy life and for that I am glad. Comfort zones never birth world changers but adversity and trial by fire makes the man.

I did not have the luxury of feeling sorry for myself or feeling entitled because the coal miners in my family looked at me with dark soot still in their eyes after a long day of digging coal miles underneath the earth. My upbringing of discomfort and hard work became my greatest asset. God used my past to give me strength. God used my struggle to help create strength.

Don't hate where you came from…it's part of your story and it helped make you the person that God has destined you to be.[5]

My American colleague in Australia, cultural commentator Bill Muehlenberg, put things in perspective for us today. He wrote, "There is nothing like a major crisis to show us what we are made of. And for the Christian, there is nothing like a major crisis to show us if we really have faith—if we have real, life-saving faith. Profession of faith is easy-peasy. Real faith that holds us up in difficult times is another matter altogether."[6]

Today COVID-19 is that crisis. He continued, "The COVID-19 crisis sure has this going for it: it is separating the fakes from those who are the real deal. It is demonstrating pretty clearly who have made Christ their rock, and those who have just gone through the motions. This sifting is one good result of this virus."[7]

And then these sobering words:

> The truth is, we have had it pretty easy in the West for a good three quarters of a century now. After WWII, we have had ever-increasing prosperity and comfort. Wars still occurred, but they were foreign wars: the Cold War, the Korean War, the Vietnam war, etc.
>
> We have been basically living the good life for quite a while now, and we are not used to hardship, deprivation and suffering. So being in a lockdown for some days now seems like the end of the world. But recall that the Great Depression stretched out for a decade, followed by the Second World War. Our parents basically knew around 15 years of extreme crisis and all that went with it.
>
> But we now think it is the end of the world if our smart phone battery dies, or if we have to wait in line more than three minutes to get our cheeseburger. So we really are a spoiled bunch in so many ways. And the sad reality is this: in times of ease and comfort, we do not need to have much faith.

> It is only as things really get tough that we start to see the need for faith.[8]

This is our time to be strong. This is our time to toughen up. This is our time to stand.

Charles Spurgeon recounts:

> In the year 1854, when I had scarcely been in London twelve months, the neighbourhood in which I laboured was visited by Asiatic cholera, and my congregation suffered from its inroads. Family after family summoned me to the bedside of the smitten, and almost every day I was called to visit the grave. I gave myself up with youthful ardour to the visitation of the sick, and was sent for from all corners of the district by persons of all ranks and religions. I became weary in body and sick at heart. My friends seemed falling one by one, and I felt or fancied that I was sickening like those around me. A little more work and weeping would have laid me low among the rest; I felt that my burden was heavier than I could bear, and I was ready to sink under it. As God would have it, I was returning mournfully home from a funeral, when my curiosity led me to read a paper which was wafered up in a shoemaker's window in the Dover Road. It did not look like a trade announcement,

nor was it, for it bore in a good bold hand-writing these words:

Because thou hast made the Lord, which is my refuge, even the most High, thy habitation; there shall no evil befall thee, neither shall any plague come nigh thy dwelling. The effect upon my heart was immediate. Faith appropriated the passage as her own. I felt secure, refreshed, girt with immortality. I went on with my visitation of the dying in a calm and peaceful spirit; I felt no fear of evil, and I suffered no harm.[9]

The words of Psalm 91 came alive to Spurgeon, enabling him to minister through exhaustion in the midst of a real plague without getting sick himself. Surely those words can speak to us today. Surely those words remain true. And surely those words can help our brothers and sisters on the front lines of health care right now, serving in the trenches at the risk of their own lives. The Lord and His promises are more than enough. (See chapter 12 and our study of Psalm 91.)

Sometimes He delivers us from crisis. Sometimes He walks with us through crisis. Sometimes He welcomes us to our heavenly home in the midst of crisis. But always He is there. And sometimes He moves in extraordinary ways, beyond our imagination. He can do that in our midst today, here and now. He remains the same forever.

John G. Lake (1870–1935) shared this striking story about his time of ministry in South Africa:

> I was ministering one time where the bubonic plague was raging. You could not hire people for a thousand dollars to bury the dead. At such times the government has to take hold of the situation. But I never took the disease.
>
> Now watch the action of the law of life. Faith belongs to the law of life. Faith is the very opposite of fear. Faith has the opposite effect in spirit, and soul, and body. Faith causes the spirit of man to become confident. It causes the mind of man to become restful, and positive. A positive mind repels disease.
>
> Consequently, the emanation of the Spirit destroys disease germs. And because we were in contact with the Spirit of life, I and a little Dutch fellow with me went out and buried many of the people who had died from the bubonic plague. We went into the homes and carried them out, dug the graves and put them in.
>
> Sometimes we would put three or four in one grave.
>
> We never took the disease. Why? Because of the knowledge that the law of life in Christ Jesus protects us. That law was

working. Because of the fact that a man by the action of his will, puts himself purposely in contact with God, faith takes possession of his heart, and the condition of his nature is changed. Instead of being fearful, he is full of faith. Instead of being absorbent and drawing everything to himself, his spirit repels sickness and disease. The Spirit of Christ Jesus flows through the whole being, and emanates through the hands, the heart, and from every pore of the body.[10]

Lake even said this:

During that great plague that I mentioned, they sent a government ship with supplies and corps of doctors. One of the doctors sent for me, and said, "What have you been using to protect yourself? Our corps has this preventative and that, which we use as protection, but we concluded that if a man could stay on the ground as you have and keep ministering to the sick and burying the dead, you must have a secret. What is it?"

I answered, "Brother that is the 'law of the Spirit of life in Christ Jesus.' I believe that just as long as I keep my soul in contact with the living God so that His Spirit is flowing into my soul and body, that no germ will ever attach itself to me, for the Spirit of God will kill it."

He asked, "Don't you think that you had better use our preventative?"

I replied, "No, but doctor I think that you would like to experiment with me.

"If you will go over to one of these dead people and take the foam that comes out of their lungs after death, then put it under the microscope you will see masses of living germs.

"You will find they are alive until a reasonable time after a man is dead. You can fill my hand with them and I will keep it under the microscope, and instead of these germs remaining alive, they will die instantly."

They tried it and found it was true. They questioned, "What is that?"

I replied, "That is 'the law of the Spirit of life in Christ Jesus.' When a man's spirit and a man's body are filled with the blessed presence of God, it oozes out of the pores of your flesh and kills the germs."[11]

This was obviously an extraordinary account, and we understand that Christians, even faith-filled Christians, can get sick or die. (It is a very rare person who lives like John Lake, and I do not recommend trying to do what he did.) But I share the account to say that even in the midst of a living hell, with corpses piling up and plagues ravaging whole communities, Jesus will make Himself real. God's life will overcome death. The Lord's people will emerge in victory, whether they live or whether they die.

In reality most of us today do not have it so badly, although some are facing the worst trials of their lifetimes. Either way it's time we take hold of God's grace, the grace that takes us over, not under; the grace that empowers our hearts and minds; the grace by which we overcome. "For everyone who has been born of God overcomes the world. And this is the victory that has overcome the world— our faith" (1 John 5:4).

Let us live, right here and right now, in this victory. The gospel was made for hard times. And so were you.

Chapter Ten

WHO OR WHAT SENT THE CORONAVIRUS? (AND DOES IT REALLY MATTER?)

D ID GOD SEND COVID-19 as a plague on
the LGBT community (or another specific
community)? Pointing to the virus-related
death of attorney Richard E. Weber, evangelical newscaster Rick Wiles said, "He was a senior
lawyer for the LGBT Bar Association of New York.
The lawyers who sue churches, the lawyers who sue
ministries...one of their senior lawyers for the gay
rights movement died today in New York City of
the coronavirus. There is a judgment, I'm telling
you, a plague is underway."[1]

But Wiles was not the only one to say something

like this (although he was certainly the most specific). As the UK newspaper *The Sun* reported, "The minister [Ralph Drollinger] who hosts a weekly Bible study for President Donald Trump's cabinet members has appeared to place blame for the coronavirus on gays and environmentalism."[2]

Drollinger explained that, "Relative to the coronavirus pandemic crisis, this is not God's abandonment wrath nor His cataclysmic wrath, rather it is sowing and reaping wrath." And *The Sun* continues, "As noted by *The Intercept*, Drollinger criticizes the 'religion of environmentalism' and people who show a 'proclivity toward lesbianism and homosexuality.'"[3]

What are we to make of such claims? Writing in the *Jerusalem Post* on March 17, Jeremy Sharon noted that

> ...a prominent ultra-Orthodox leader, Rabbi Meir Mazuz, proffered a similar and more specific explanation to Aviner's. He claimed that the LGBTQ community and Gay Pride marches were against nature and had caused the coronavirus pandemic.
>
> And Mazuz is not the only cleric to have made such accusations.
>
> Pastor Steven Andrew of the USA Christian Church designated the month of March as "Repent of LGBT Sin Month," and

said that "obeying God protects the USA from diseases, such as the coronavirus."[4]

It's understandable that the secular world would mock words like this, especially the very specific statement of Rick Wiles. Yet when reading through Rev. Drollinger's Bible study in full, he takes time to go through the Scriptures, noting how complex the issue of divine judgment is when applied directly to a nation or people.[5] He also looks carefully at the divine judgments in Romans 1, as God gave us over to our sins, and he equates our extreme environmentalism with idolatry, also noting the emphasis Romans 1 puts on homosexual practice. But does that mean that COVID-19 is a specific, direct judgment from God on extreme environmentalists and gays? As for the latter, Wiles says that the answer is yes.

But what would Wiles say about pastors who have died of the virus? Or children who have died?[6] Was this divine judgment on them? As I mentioned earlier, the first coronavirus casualty in Oklahoma was a Pentecostal pastor, presumably a man who viewed homosexual practice as sinful. Why then did he die? An elderly pastor who attended John MacArthur's recent leadership conference in California has apparently died of the virus.[7] Yet he too presumably opposed LGBT activism. And what do we make of headlines like this: "Coronavirus strikes pastor, wife and over 30 others at Ark. church"?[8]

We need to be very careful when we speak of divine judgment, since in God's sight all of us are worthy of judgment and wrath. We stand by mercy more than merit.

To be sure, the Scriptures are clear that God is a righteous judge, and there are times when He pours out His wrath on the earth. (See chapter 11 for more on this.) And sometimes He judges us by giving us over to our sins, as stated in Romans 1. Based on this passage, I do see evidence of God's judgment in our society, as we have turned from God to idols (of many kinds), then to sexual immorality, then to homosexuality, then to many other sins. As Paul sums things up (speaking not of America but of the history of the human race):

> Furthermore, just as they did not think it worthwhile to retain the knowledge of God, so God gave them over to a depraved mind, so that they do what ought not to be done. They have become filled with every kind of wickedness, evil, greed and depravity. They are full of envy, murder, strife, deceit and malice. They are gossips, slanderers, God-haters, insolent, arrogant and boastful; they invent ways of doing evil; they disobey their parents; they have no understanding, no fidelity, no love, no mercy. Although they

know God's righteous decree that those
who do such things deserve death, they not
only continue to do these very things but
also approve of those who practice them.

—ROMANS 1:28–32

But a light goes on when you read a passage like
this. Rather than pointing the finger at others—
those evil gays or those terrible atheists—Paul
points the finger at the human race as a whole,
which includes you and me, outside of grace. We
are all guilty and worthy of judgment. These words
describe all of us.

Jesus addressed this in Luke 13, where we read,

Now there were some present at that time
who told Jesus about the Galileans whose
blood Pilate had mixed with their sacrifices.
Jesus answered, "Do you think that these
Galileans were worse sinners than all the
other Galileans because they suffered this
way? I tell you, no! But unless you repent,
you too will all perish. Or those eighteen
who died when the tower in Siloam fell on
them—do you think they were more guilty
than all the others living in Jerusalem? I tell
you, no! But unless you repent, you too will
all perish."

—LUKE 13:1–5

WHEN THE WORLD STOPS

Do you see what the Lord is saying? It's easy to look at someone who died an unusual death, or a sudden death, or a gruesome death, and say, "Obviously, he deserved it," or, "She got what was coming to her." Jesus says, "Not so!" All of us, outside of His grace, are habitual sinners, and all of us, outside of His mercy, are worthy of judgment, both in this world and in the world to come.

Of course, there *are* times when God brings judgment on sinning individuals, such as Nadab and Abihu in the Old Testament (see Leviticus 10:1–3) or Ananias and Sapphira in the New Testament (see Acts 5:1–11). There *are* times when God singles out a sinning person for a specific act of disobedience, like Uzzah in the Old Testament (see 2 Samuel 6:1–8) or Herod in the New Testament (see Acts 12:21–23).

But in the vast majority of cases, we do best to be slow to speak and slow to judge. As Paul wrote to the Romans (immediately after the verses I just cited), "You, therefore, have no excuse, you who pass judgment on someone else, for at whatever point you judge another, you are condemning yourself, because you who pass judgment do the same things" (Rom. 2:1). That old saying remains true: when we point one finger at others, we have three fingers pointing back at us.

Can God give specific revelation to His people, explaining that something is a judgment from His hand? Absolutely, and we should take that seriously, especially if the person speaking has a reliable, proven track record. For example, some contemporary prophets believe that God has revealed to them why the virus started in China and has had such a devastating impact in Italy and Iran. (Consider these statements from Jeremiah Johnson.[9]) We can weigh those words carefully and prayerfully.

And there are some leaders, such as Pastor Ed Silvoso, who believe that there is an important divine message in the coronavirus. He said, "'The darkness covering the Earth, in my estimation, is not demonic in origin. It's God dimming the lights in the theater' before shining a spotlight on the church, 'so that the eyes of the world will turn toward those that have become the light of the world because they carry Jesus in their heart.'"[10]

Other leaders, such as prayer leader Lou Engle, feel the virus *is* demonic in origin, stating, "It is our conviction that the storm of this pandemic has been stirred up by a high-level demonic principality to hinder the surge of the Church's mighty assault of fasting, prayer, sending and missions on the global gates of Hades."[11] Specifically, with so many significant Christian stadium events planned for 2020, the virus is a demonic attempt to thwart those major gatherings.

How do we sort this out? What do we do when major respected leaders have different insights about the origins of the virus or the purpose of the virus? Did God send it in judgment? Did Satan send it to stop revival? Or is it something entirely man-made, created by human hands in a factory? (I saw a video where one prophet said that in a vision he saw people making the virus in a lab in China.) Or is it an entirely natural phenomenon, as many scientists believe, saying they have conclusive evidence that COVID-19 was not produced by man?[12]

There are also the conspiracy theories about the real origins or alleged nefarious purposes of the virus, and they are growing by the minute. There are YouTube videos making some of the most outrageous claims about the virus, and they have been watched millions of times. When I asked my social media followers on Facebook and Twitter to list for me some of the oddest theories they had heard, I got a flood of responses, including:

- That this was a dry run to test responsiveness. Bill Gates & his involvement in Event201, his focus on overpopulation and vaccines, digital tracking, tanking of dollar, etc.

- Some "scientist" reportedly suggests the source of the COVID-19 virus was a meteor.

- Chinese and US nanotechnology infiltrated people via forced Chinese vaccines and US chemtrails and those governments can control whether we live or die as part of a multi-government population control initiative.

- A foreigner living in China heard a local say she read in the news that it was engineered in an American lab and one of the Chinese employees accidentally caught it and brought it back home with her.

- Two-hundred generals hatched this plot in the aftermath of 9/11, with a goal of destroying pedophile rings.

- A feminist lawmaker is claiming that the coronavirus is a "weapon of the patriarchy," even though the virus is killing more men than women.

- There will be a chip in the vaccine, preparing the way for a one-world government and, ultimately, the antichrist. And if you do some mathematical equation with the word COVID, it creates the number 666.

- The European Union would be involved along with progressive politicians in order to reduce internal social expenditure, solve the aging population problem and repopulate Europe with Islamic immigration in order to satisfy anti-Semitic internal movements. Besides stopping Trump.

- The virus is somehow connected to Satanists in Hollywood who are sacrificing babies to the devil.

- Leftists are in cahoots with China to ruin our economy and take down Trump so he won't be re-elected.

- The Imam in Syracuse, NY said CoViD-19 is Allah's judgement on us because women show too much ankle.

- It started with people eating bats in Wuhan.

- It's an engineered virus based on a known bat virus to ensure China can use [it] to leverage US trade. Goes along with their current stranglehold on prescription medications much needed by the US. Also, the main stream media has now got their message to NOT use racist "Chinese virus" headlines.

- The virus was "designed" to sterilize men since it attacks the RNA. Since women have XX, and immunity capability is with that chromosome, women have a better chance of recovery than men.

- That the U.S. or Israel created it (quite a popular propaganda message from Chinese and Iranian sources, obviously Iran accusing Israel and China accusing U.S.; and of course, the Jews will always get blamed for causing a pandemic).

- That George Soros created it and that China did it to reduce population.

- The virus was created to reduce global population because Earth's resources can only sustain a certain amount of people. And that it targets older people and immuno-suppressed people to make sure the fittest survive the pandemic.

- The virus was created to be a distraction for an asteroid about to hit Earth and cause total annihilation. The idea is that by creating this distraction and forced shutdown, it keeps people off the streets and unable to create massive civil unrest and keep families together until the end, as well.

- The virus was a coverup for those who were either under house arrest (Canadian PM Trudeau) or in witness protection who will testify (Tom Hanks) in conjunction with the Jeffrey Epstein case.[13]

And on and on it goes, as this list is just a sampling of the responses I received on social media and on my daily radio broadcast, *The Line of Fire*,[14] which in turn represents just a sampling of what is "out there" these days—and yes, some of what is out there is really out there!

But for me it's all very simple, even though I don't know: if the virus was entirely natural in its origins, or if it was manufactured by people, or if it's a natural phenomenon and people are trying to manipulate it for their purposes, or if it's a demonic attack on both believer and unbeliever, or if it's divine judgment on specific locations and cities or on the whole, or if it's a combination of any of the above.

I do not have the ability to investigate every theory (in fact no one does, which is why there can be so many theories; who can disprove them all?). And the Spirit of God has not chosen to reveal to me the origins of the virus. But honestly I don't need to know any of these things. I simply need to know 1) what God is doing in the midst of the pandemic; and 2) how He wants us, as His people, to respond.

In that regard I can believe these things with confidence:

- God is using this virus as a wake-up call to His people and to the nations, as I explained in chapter 6. It is high time that we pray and cry out for mercy. It is high time we repent of our sins. Whoever sent the virus, whatever caused the virus, the Lord is getting the attention of the world through it. This is not happening without His explicit permission.

- In the virus is a divine invitation to us to seek Him earnestly and to reevaluate how we live and how we function as the church. (See chapters 6 and 7.) When else will we have an opportunity forced on us like this, shut up in our homes, with no sports and normal social outlets? This unique moment also calls us to live in the light of eternity and to recognize what really matters, sharing the good news with others. This is a great time for the harvest![15]

- Third, and closely related, the virus
  offers us a platform to shine the
  light of the gospel and to live differ-
  ently than the world. These are divine
  opportunities! As Bishop Joseph
  Mattera wrote,

The present coronavirus pandemic will demonstrate how the Kingdom of God is different from the kingdom of darkness. It is also a huge opportunity for the church to function as the Salt and Light of the world. The reason is because the Kingdom of the heavens is governed by a different set of laws and principles than those under the rule of the prince of this world. (See John 14:30, 1 John 5:19.)

The first example he gave was this:

Instead of hoarding goods, we are generous with others. While Christians should save money and food to provide for their imme- diate family, our mindset should be to also have enough to provide for our community. Many great leaders I know in the Body of Christ are always champions during times of crisis and utilize their church buildings and vast resources to provide food, medical care, and much needed intervention for their communities and cities.[16]

In the words of Catherine Booth, "You are not here in the world for yourself. You have been sent here for others. The world is waiting for you!"[17]

- The virus will uncover what is in our hearts, be it faith or fear, generosity or greed, consecration or carnality, courage or cowardice. In times of shaking, we see what is real and what is not.

- Sudden, radical world changes remind us that things can turn on a dime, that prophecy can be fulfilled suddenly, and that life as we know it can be turned upside down. All the more reason for us to put our roots deep down into God. All the more reason for us to *know* the Lord rather than just know *about* Him.

- The virus reminds us of the frailty of human life, of how quickly life can be taken from us, of how fragile the elderly can be. We do well to cherish every day we have and to honor and care for those who are weak among us.

I believe the Spirit is saying that old lives matter too. (See chapter 8.)

- The present temporary shaking of the world provides a foretaste of the final, massive, overwhelming shaking that will come, a shaking so intense that only the kingdom of God will remain unshaken. Are we ready for that day? (See chapter 11.)

In the Book of Job, while we are given insight into the wager between God and Satan that caused him such horrific suffering, Job himself is never given that insight. Even in the end of the book, when the Lord reveals Himself to Job, He never explains things to Job. Instead, He reveals Himself—His majesty, His glory, His sovereignty, His power—and that is enough for godly Job. As he said to the Lord, "My ears had heard of you but now my eyes have seen you" (Job 42:5).

That will be enough for us too, even if we never know exactly who or what was behind this current pandemic (or the next one that might come). Instead, if we encounter God afresh, if we experience Him more deeply, if we turn from our carnal ways and truly seek Him, if we turn our focus from selfishness to service, that will be enough for us—more than enough.

And through it all, come thick or thin, we proclaim

with boldness and joy that JESUS IS LORD. He is always more than enough. People may have their purposes and plans, from governments to companies, and there may even be some truth to a conspiracy theory here or there. But in the end only God's purposes and plans will stand, and if we align ourselves with Him, all will be well. Stand firm!

Chapter Eleven

ONE DAY EVERYTHING
WILL BE SHAKEN

IT'S TRUE THAT the coronavirus has caused upheaval around the world. Whole countries have been quarantined. Massive sports events have been canceled. (Even the Olympics have been postponed.) Universities have been closed. The stock markets have jumped and plunged down like a yo-yo. Millions have lost their jobs. Tens of thousands have lost their lives. But this is a mere tremor compared with what is coming. One day the whole earth will be shaken.

As the author of Hebrews tells us, the Lord "has promised, 'Once more I will shake not only the earth but also the heavens.' The words 'once more' indicate the removing of what can be shaken—that is, created things—so that what cannot be shaken may remain" (Heb. 12:26–27). Everything will be shaken on that day.

This is how Jesus described it: "There will be signs in the sun, moon and stars. On the earth, nations will be in anguish and perplexity at the roaring and tossing of the sea. People will faint from terror, apprehensive of what is coming on the world, for the heavenly bodies will be shaken" (Luke 21:25–26).

Or, in the vivid language of the Book of Revelation,

> Then the kings of the earth, the princes, the generals, the rich, the mighty, and everyone else, both slave and free, hid in caves and among the rocks of the mountains. They called to the mountains and the rocks, "Fall on us and hide us from the face of him who sits on the throne and from the wrath of the Lamb! For the great day of their wrath has come, and who can withstand it?"
> —REVELATION 6:15–17

Can you even imagine a scene like this?

Very few want to talk about God's judgment today, even within the church. Preachers choose to avoid it, and the congregants cheer them on. "Give us sweet stuff! Give us happy stuff! Tell us nice stories. Make us smile! We don't want to hear about judgment. That makes God sound mean."

To the contrary, that makes God sound just. He *will* judge unrighteousness. He *will* punish the wicked. He *will* bring retribution. That is good news for the righteous and the godly. As the psalmist said, "Let all creation rejoice before the LORD, for he comes, he comes to judge the earth. He will judge the world in righteousness and the peoples in his faithfulness" (Ps. 96:13). Judgment on the wicked also means salvation for the righteous.

The Book of Revelation also speaks of the pouring out of seven bowls of divine wrath on the earth, resulting in horrific judgments on those who refuse to repent. (See Revelation 16.) There will be no vaccines or cures on that day. There will be no intervention by the federal government. There will be no way of escape—other than running to the Lord for mercy and taking refuge under His wings. Judgment is certainly coming! And to repeat, it will be an act of justice from the Lord.

Listen to these words from Revelation 16:

> Then I heard a loud voice from the temple saying to the seven angels, "Go, pour out the seven bowls of God's wrath on the earth."
>
> The first angel went and poured out his bowl on the land, and ugly, festering sores broke out on the people who had the mark of the beast and worshiped its image.
>
> The second angel poured out his bowl on

the sea, and it turned into blood like that of a dead person, and every living thing in the sea died.

The third angel poured out his bowl on the rivers and springs of water, and they became blood.

Then I heard the angel in charge of the waters say: "You are just in these judgments, O Holy One, you who are and who were; for they have shed the blood of your holy people and your prophets, and you have given them blood to drink as they deserve."

And I heard the altar respond: "Yes, Lord God Almighty, true and just are your judgments."

—REVELATION 16:1–7

Yes, Lord, your judgments are true and just! Isaiah described it like this (please read this slowly and prayerfully):

See, the LORD is going to lay waste the earth and devastate it; he will ruin its face and scatter its inhabitants—it will be the same for priest as for people, for the master as for his servant, for the mistress as for her servant, for seller as for buyer, for borrower as for lender, for debtor as for creditor. The earth will be completely laid waste and totally plundered. The LORD has spoken this word.

The earth dries up and withers, the world languishes and withers, the heavens languish with the earth. The earth is defiled by its people; they have disobeyed the laws, violated the statutes and broken the everlasting covenant. Therefore a curse consumes the earth; its people must bear their guilt. Therefore earth's inhabitants are burned up, and very few are left.

—ISAIAH 24:1–6

Even if we understand that the prophets sometimes spoke in hyperbolic language, the overall meaning of these words is undeniable: one day severe judgment will fall on a guilty planet. Yet even in the midst of this terrifying description, there are words of hope for God's people. In fact, there is a divine invitation to take refuge in Him:

Go, my people, enter your rooms and shut the doors behind you; hide yourselves for a little while until his wrath has passed by. See, the LORD is coming out of his dwelling to punish the people of the earth for their sins. The earth will disclose the blood shed on it; the earth will conceal its slain no longer.

—ISAIAH 26:20–21

The Lord will provide a place of refuge and safety in the midst of the intense judgment storm. As Proverbs states, "The name of the LORD is a fortified tower; the righteous run to it and are safe" (Prov. 18:10). And as Psalm 91 declares, there is a place of protection, a hiding place, in God Most High. (See chapter 12 for an exposition of this psalm based on the Hebrew text.)

That's why Jesus said this to His followers, immediately after warning of the judgment that would be coming to the earth: "When these things begin to take place, stand up and lift up your heads, because your redemption is drawing near" (Luke 21:28). The coming of the Lord is at hand. And that's why the very passage from Hebrews that we quoted at the beginning of this chapter ends with this: "Therefore, since we are receiving a kingdom that cannot be shaken, let us be thankful, and so worship God acceptably with reverence and awe, for our 'God is a consuming fire'" (Heb. 12:28–29).

The whole world will be shaken, but God's kingdom—and God's people—will not be shaken. As the psalmist declared,

> God is our refuge and strength, an ever-present help in trouble. Therefore we will not fear, though the earth give way and the mountains fall into the heart of the sea, though its waters roar and foam and the

mountains quake with their surging. There is a river whose streams make glad the city of God, the holy place where the Most High dwells. God is within her, she will not fall; God will help her at break of day.

—PSALM 46:1–5

What amazing words! Even with mountains crashing into the sea and the whole earth quaking, *we will not fear.*

As the psalmist also wrote:

Surely the righteous will never be shaken; they will be remembered forever. They will have no fear of bad news; their hearts are steadfast, trusting in the LORD. Their hearts are secure, they will have no fear; in the end they will look in triumph on their foes.

—PSALM 112:6–8

It is true that the coronavirus has taken many lives so far, and every life is precious. And it is true that many more lives could be lost, along with ongoing suffering and hardship for hundreds of millions due to economic crises. But this is only a small blip on the radar compared with what is coming.

Now would be a good time for us, as God's holy people, to learn to trust Him in the midst of crisis, putting our spiritual roots down deep. Now would be a good time to realize that all life is transitory and that at best we are only passing through this world. Now would be a good time to take hold afresh of the beauty of the cross and the gift of eternal life. And now would be a good time to be used as agents of mercy and hope to a hurting world. In Jesus we have all that we will ever need. And in Him we will never be shaken.

A GOD OF JUSTICE AND MERCY

But we cannot stop here when speaking of the acts of God, although it is absolutely true that our God is a righteous judge who will one day pour out His wrath on a rebellious world. Yet the overwhelming emphasis of Scripture is not on the wrath of God but rather on His mercy. As the psalmist proclaimed, "The LORD is compassionate and gracious, slow to anger, abounding in love" (Ps. 103:8).

Can you imagine if God's character were the opposite of this? If He were slow to show mercy and abounding in anger? We would have been wiped out many millennia ago.

As the psalmist continued,

> He will not always accuse, nor will he harbor
> his anger forever; he does not treat us as our
> sins deserve or repay us according to our
> iniquities. For as high as the heavens are
> above the earth, so great is his love for those
> who fear him; as far as the east is from the

west, so far has he removed our transgres-
sions from us. As a father has compassion
on his children, so the LORD has compassion on those who fear him; for he knows
how we are formed, he remembers that we
are dust.

—PSALM 103:9–14

What wonderful, encouraging, life-giving words. Who could imagine an all-powerful God who could be so gentle and kind? And remember, these words were written long before the cross. Long before God displayed His love for us through His Son. Long before the perfect Savior paid for our sins. Yet the psalmist, David himself, understood the greatness of God's mercy and kindness and compassion and longsuffering. That is who our God is.

The prophet Micah, who had much to say about divine judgment, also said this about the Lord: "Who is a God like you, who pardons sin and for-gives the transgression of the remnant of his inheri-tance? You do not stay angry forever but delight to show mercy" (Mic. 7:18). Our God delights to show mercy.

Similarly, the prophet Ezekiel, who too prophe-sied about the judgment of God, said this on behalf of the Lord: "Rid yourselves of all the offenses you have committed, and get a new heart and a new spirit. Why will you die, people of Israel? For I take no pleasure in the death of anyone, declares the Sovereign LORD. Repent and live!" (Ezek. 18:31–32). Yes, our righteous God looks for opportunities to show mercy. He desires to demonstrate His compassion. And while He will not overlook our rebellion and sin—that is, if we refuse to turn away from it—He is longing to forgive.

The Book of Genesis contains a remarkable dialogue between the Lord and Abraham, related as a face-to-face conversation between the two. (See Genesis 18:16–33.) In the account we learn that the Lord is about to destroy the cities of Sodom and Gomorrah because of their wickedness. But Abraham's nephew, Lot, lives in Sodom, along with his wife and children. So God, in His incredible condescension, wants to let Abraham know in advance, prompting Abraham to take a bold step in faith.

As Genesis records,

> Then Abraham approached him and said: "Will you sweep away the righteous with the wicked? What if there are fifty righteous people in the city? Will you really sweep it away and not spare the place for the sake of the fifty righteous people in it? Far be it from you to do such a thing—to kill the righteous with the wicked, treating the righteous and the wicked alike. Far be it

from you! Will not the Judge of all the earth
do right?"

—Genesis 18:23–25

What an extraordinary prayer. And what an outrageous appeal. To paraphrase, "God, I know that
You have every right to judge these places, but You
are a righteous judge. And that means You won't
destroy the innocent along with the guilty. So if
You find fifty righteous people there, will You spare
the whole population?" Remarkably, the Lord—the
Creator and sustainer of the universe—acceded to
Abraham's request: "I will spare the city for the sake
of the fifty."

But Abraham wasn't done. "What if there are
forty-five righteous?" "I'll spare it" was the reply.
"How about forty?" Abraham was really going out
on a limb! Amazingly the Lord said yes to that
request as well. In fact, He said yes to every one of
Abraham's requests, which ended with God agreeing
to spare the entire city of Sodom if He could find
just ten righteous people in it. Sadly, He could not,
so judgment was poured out.

Yet we get an incredible glimpse into God's heart
toward His creation. He will bend over backward
to withhold judgment. He will give us every chance
to repent. He will be incredibly longsuffering and
patient. Only then will His wrath be poured out.

The ultimate proof of this is found in the cross.

There, rather than God pouring out His judgment on all of us—yes, all are guilty sinners in His sight—He poured out judgment on His Son. Jesus took our place. Jesus bore our guilt. Jesus paid for our sins. That is the heart of the gospel. That is the heart of God.

As we pray then for the Lord's intervention in the midst of the current world crisis, let us appeal to His mercy and compassion. God alone knows what caused this viral outbreak, and God alone can dramatically turn the tide. Even the *Wall Street Journal* has recognized the potential of the moment, writing on March 26, "Could a plague of biblical proportions be America's best hope for religious revival? As the 75th anniversary of the end of World War II approaches, there is reason to think so."[1] This is in the *Wall Street Journal*!

The article, by Robert Nicholson, president of the Philos Project, closes with this: "Could a rogue virus lead to a grand creative moment in America's history? Will Americans, shaken by the reality of a risky universe, rediscover the God who proclaimed himself sovereign over every catastrophe?"[2]

May the whole world awaken to this reality! And so we pray,

> *Have mercy on us, O Lord, and grant us repentance from our sins. We have no hope outside of You.*

Intervene, our God, in the midst of this crisis with grace and healing and deliverance, and let the world know that You are a prayer-answering God. Yes, let the whole world know!

And send a glorious revival to Your church, leading to a massive awakening in our land.

May our nation be ablaze with the gospel. May we see the greatest harvest in our history. May Your people arise and shine!

It is time, Lord God, it is time! May Jesus be exalted in our day!

Chapter Twelve

PSALM 91: LIVING IN THE HIDING PLACE OF THE MOST HIGH

YOU MAY BE reading this book in April 2020, right in the midst of the swirling COVID-19 storm. Or you may be reading this book one year later, or five years later, when the challenges we face are very different. And yet all of us, at all times and in all places, need to take hold of the holy reality of Psalm 91 since we live in a dangerous world filled with demons, disease, and death. So we close this book with a message of lasting relevance as we focus on the message of this glorious psalm.

In truth there is nothing in the Bible like Psalm 91. Yet we don't know who wrote it or when it was written (although Jewish tradition ascribes it to Moses), and it has multiple speakers (including the Lord). More importantly, it is unique in its scope and promises, composed in Old Testament times and yet anticipating New Testament realities. And it has unique relevance during seasons of plague, pestilence, and pandemic. Let's go through it verse by verse, opening up the riches of the Hebrew text.

Jewish tradition believes Moses wrote this psalm, since he is the author of Psalm 90, leading to speculation that he wrote Psalm 91 as well. While it's not impossible, we have no evidence Moses did write it. But whoever wrote it, God inspired it, and it is a sacred part of the Scriptures. Not only so, but its scope is universal: it applies to anyone and to everyone who will live by its guidelines, follow its directives, and take hold of its promises.

It sets before us a vision, a possibility, an ideal. And though the realities of Psalm 91 may seem unattainable, they are here to invite us, not to frustrate us; to encourage rather than condemn. Let us find this hiding place in Jesus, and let us learn to live there.

Verse 1: "Whoever dwells in the shelter of the Most High will rest in the shadow of the Almighty."

We're going to spend a lot of time on this first verse, since it lays the foundation for everything that follows. The opening Hebrew word is *yoshev*, which is an active participle. This refers to continuous action, to life habit, to what one does all the time. Used as a noun, *yoshev* can refer to someone who lives in a particular place, as in, "I'm an inhabitant of New York City." So Psalm 91 is giving promises to someone who lives in God's shelter and protection. Put another way, if I asked you, "Where do you live?" your answer would be, "I live in the shelter of the Most High."

But there's more to that Hebrew word for *shelter*, which is *seter*. It is not just a shelter; it is a hiding place, a covert, a secret refuge. It is found in verses including Isaiah 32:2, which says, "Each one will be like a *shelter* from the wind and a refuge from the storm, like streams of water in the desert and the shadow of a great rock in a thirsty land" (Isa. 32:2, emphasis added). It is also found in verses including 1 Samuel 19:2, when Saul is threatening to kill David and which emphasize the aspect of "hiding place, secret place" even more: "And Jonathan told David, 'Saul my father seeks to kill you. Therefore be on your guard in the morning. Stay in a *secret place* and hide yourself'" (ESV, emphasis added).

This is where God is calling us to live. In that hiding place, that divine shelter, that secret place where no one can touch us and nothing can harm us. And even though that place is spiritual rather than physical, it is even more real than a physical shelter or hiding place. The Lord Himself is impregnable.

You see, this is not just the hiding place of any god or higher power. This is the hiding place of the *Most High God*, a term that is found dozens of times in the Old Testament, especially in the psalms (starting in Ps. 7:17) and Daniel (where the one true God is contrasted with the false gods of the nations, starting in Dan. 3:26). It is also expressed in the Song of Moses in Exodus 15:11: "Who among the gods is like you, LORD? Who is like you—majestic in holiness, awesome in glory, working wonders?"

There may be other so-called gods and powers, but there is none like our God. He alone is eternal. He alone is immortal. He alone is omnipotent and omniscient and omnipresent. He is the Most High God, the only one worthy of being called God. Even the demons understand this, crying out to Jesus in the New Testament, "What do you want with me, Jesus, Son of the Most High God? In God's name don't torture me!" (Mark 5:7; see also Acts 16:17). In fact, when Gabriel announces to Miriam (Mary) that she will give birth to the Messiah, he says, "He will be great and will be called the Son of the Most High. The Lord God will give him the throne of his father David" (Luke 1:32). This psalm is for those who live in His divine shelter, in His hiding place.

The second half of verse 1 describes this person as someone who regularly spends the night lodging in the shadow of Shaddai, normally translated "Almighty." And while scholars debate the exact meaning of the word, it seems that the aspects of power and provision are clearly associated with Shaddai. As for *shadow*, this image speaks of covering as well as refreshing, a place away from the heat of the day.

Verse 2: "I will say of the LORD, 'He is my refuge and my fortress, my God, in whom I trust.'"

Now an unnamed individual speaks, but the intent is that it could be you or me. Let these be your words and mine! So say this about Yahweh (Jehovah), the only true God. He is *your* refuge, the safe place to which you run and hide where the enemy cannot find you. He is *your* fortress, that impregnable place where the enemy cannot touch you. He is *your* God, and you place your trust in Him.

Verse 3: "For he will deliver you from the snare of the fowler and from the deadly pestilence" (ESV).

This verse indicates that we are still living in a dangerous world, even while we live in God's hiding place. In other words, He doesn't take us out of the world but rather delivers us from evil and disaster while we live in this world. This is in harmony with the Lord's prayer for the apostles in John 17:15: "My prayer is not that you take them out of the world but that you protect them from the evil one" (John 17:15).

Just as a bird hunter puts out his snare (Hebrew *pakh* is a trapper's net), the enemy will set traps for us, including destructive plagues. But our God will deliver us.

Verse 4: "He will cover you with his pinions, and under his wings you will find refuge; his faithfulness is a shield and buckler" (ESV).

Here the image changes to that of a protective bird—pointing to God's personal and gentle care for us—with His faithfulness serving as a large shield and a small shield (or a shield and protective wall; see NET). We stand in His truth, and we are safe.

Verses 5–6: "You will not fear the terror of night, nor the arrow that flies by day, nor the pestilence that stalks in the darkness, nor the plague that destroys at midday."

The Hebrew word *pakhad* can refer to a fear or to the thing feared (as in something fearful), translated here as "terror." Dwelling in that holy hiding place, we do not fear the nighttime terrors, which seem especially frightful, or the daytime arrows—yes, demons and people are out to get us! We don't even fear the pestilence (Hebrew *dever*, which was used in verse 3) or the plague (Hebrew *qetev*), which some even take as the name of a demon, as it comes stalking during the middle of the day. Yet still we have no fear, despite flying arrows, menacing plagues, and all kinds of terrors at night. No fear!

Verses 7–8: "A thousand may fall at your side, ten thousand at your right hand, but it will not come near you. You will only observe with your eyes and see the punishment of the wicked."

This underscores the reality of the promises. People *are* dying—by the thousands all around us, as in a terrible time of war or epidemic—yet death does not touch us. To the contrary, we will only see God's judgment wipe out the wicked (which describes those who are dying all around us).

To be clear, these verses are not saying that if one person dies during a plague and the other does not, you can conclude that the one who lived was righteous and the one who died was wicked. The Book of Job urges us not to think that way. But these verses *are* saying two things. First, if you love the Lord and walk with Him, when He pours out judgment on the wicked, it will not touch you. Second, even if others are dying in plagues and battles, in that hiding place you will be secure.

Verses 9–10: "Because you have made the LORD your dwelling place—the Most High, who is my refuge—no evil shall be allowed to befall you, no plague come near your tent" (ESV).

Now the psalmist speaks directly, addressing each of us personally—that is, addressing those of us who have taken shelter in the Lord. He describes Yahweh here again as the Most High, speaking of Him in the first person as "my refuge," just as we did in verse 2. And he describes us as those who have made Him our dwelling place (Hebrew *ma'ohn*), a word found in Psalm 90 as well, where Moses wrote, "Lord, you have been our dwelling place throughout all generations" (Ps. 90:1).

To say it again, this is where we live—or, better yet, *He* is where we live. So if someone were to ask you, "Where do you live?" you could even answer, "I live in the Most High!" Consequently, no evil will befall us (the Hebrew *ra'ah* speaks of evil or disaster) and no plague—here the word *nega'*, which speaks of something that afflicts or strikes us—will come near our tent, implying our family as well.

Verses 11–12: "For he will command his angels concerning you to guard you in all your ways; they will lift you up in their hands, so that you will not strike your foot against a stone."

This supernatural protection comes about as a result of God sending His angels to guard us wherever we go, lifting us up so we don't even smash our foot against a rock. What amazing care! As it is written in Psalm 34:7, "The angel of the LORD encamps around those who fear him, and he delivers them." Nothing can get past the angel of the Lord.

Verse 13: "You will tread on the lion and the cobra; you will trample the great lion and the serpent."

This verse anticipates the authority we have as believers in the New Testament, underlying these words of Jesus in Luke 10:19: "I have given you authority to trample on snakes and scorpions and to overcome all the power of the enemy; nothing will harm you." Here, even in a pre-cross, pre-resurrection context, the believer who lives in Yahweh can trample these foes underfoot, described here in vivid physical terms and likened to dangerous lions and deadly snakes.

The Hebrew *peten*, translated here as "cobra," can speak more broadly of a venomous snake, while Hebrew *shakhal*, rendered "great lion" in the NIV, might refer to the young lion. As for the word translated "serpent," Hebrew *tannin*, in other verses it speaks of a crocodile, a sea-monster, or a dragon. Whatever it is, it is under our feet!

Verse 14: "Because he loves me," says the LORD, "I will rescue him; I will protect him, for he acknowledges my name."

Now the Lord Himself speaks, sharing His heart and His perspective. And what matters most to Him? That we love Him! But this is not the normal Hebrew word for love. Instead, it is *khashaq*, which speaks of a loving attachment to someone, as expressed well in the ESV: "Because he holds fast to me in love." Yes! Others render with "clings to me" (NJV) or "has his heart set on me" (CSB) or "has devoted his love to Me" (TLV).

Because of that, Yahweh promises to rescue us, a recurring theme in this psalm, and because we know (or acknowledge) His name, He will protect us, by setting us on high, where we are out of danger. And what does it mean to "acknowledge His name"? In the words of Charles Spurgeon, "The man has known the attributes of God so as to trust in him, and then by experience has arrived at a yet deeper knowledge, this shall be regarded by the Lord as a pledge of his grace, and he will set the owner of it above danger or fear, where he shall dwell in peace and joy."[1]

Verse 15: "He will call on me, and I will answer him; I will be with him in trouble, I will deliver him and honor him."

Take a moment to grasp what God—the almighty Creator and King—is saying here. Because of the intimacy we enjoy with Him, because we know and honor Him, He in turn will honor us. Yes, *God* will honor *us*! When we call to Him, He will be near, hearing us and answering us. And when we go through times of trouble—Hebrew *tsarah*, which the Septuagint, the ancient Greek translation, renders with *thlipsis*, tribulation (used also in John

16:33 and Acts 14:22, already quoted in this book)—
He will be right there with us to help and deliver.

And yes, the Lord says He will honor us, using the
exact same word in Hebrew (*kabbed*) that is used
in the Ten Commandments, where we are called to
honor our father and mother. To say it once more
(since it is so amazing, beyond human comprehen-
sion), when we live in Him and devote our love to
Him, He will honor us.

**Verse 16: "With long life I will satisfy him and
show him my salvation."**

The Hebrew reads just as the English, giving a
promise of long life, which is found throughout
the Old Testament in conjunction with obedience.
(See, for example, Exodus 23:25–26; Proverbs 3:1–
2.) Yet here, uniquely, God says He will *satisfy* us
with that life, meaning it will be a blessed life, a
life enriched by Him. And He will show us His salvation (Hebrew *y'shuah*), a word used quite holis-
tically in the Hebrew Scriptures, speaking of both
physical and spiritual deliverance. God will make it
real in our lives! And this long life will, ultimately,
last forever.

* * *

Can you see now why I said that Psalm 91 is so
unique and so special? And be assured that *every
word written in this psalm is true*. It is not just

hyperbole. It is not just exaggerated speech. It is divine truth. These are divine promises.

"But," you say, "I don't see anyone experiencing what is promised here!"

To some extent that is true, since very few of us take up the divine invitation. Very few of us *really* determine to live like this long term. On the other hand, to the extent we can take hold of these promises, to the extent we can experience them, and in times of pandemic and crisis and fear we should repeat this psalm throughout the day.

As for how to live in that place of divine shelter and refuge, here are four simple keys: First, do your best to put down deep, spiritual roots by spending quality time with the Lord every day, in particular in prayer and the Word. This is where we put our stake in the ground, so to say. This is where we lay our foundations. This is what helps us keep our bearings when things get rough (and be assured that, at one time or another in all our lives, things will get rough).

Second, throughout the day seek to cultivate a consciousness of God, talking with Him, thanking Him, reflecting on Him, inviting Him to be with you, even having Him with you 24/7 as your companion and friend, as if He was right there with you, whatever you're doing, looking over your shoulder, standing next to you. (In reality, He is much nearer than that.) Also, wherever possible incorporate worship into your day, since worship brings the presence of God. And consider this principle as well: if you can be *worried* throughout the day when something is wrong, no matter what you're doing, you can be *God conscious* throughout the day, no matter what you're doing. (An old friend of mine once suggested that we "worry the Word"!)

Third, determine to walk in obedience to His ways, maintaining fellowship by living in truth. Holiness is nonnegotiable, and sin in our spirits is far more deadly than COVID-19 in our lungs. And if you sin and fall short, turn to Him instantly in repentance, asking for (and receiving!) His cleansing and washing. Then go back to loving on Him and pursuing holiness rather than wallowing in guilt. As 1 John states, "But if we walk in the light, as he is in the light, we have fellowship with one another, and the blood of Jesus, his Son, purifies us from all sin" (1 John 1:7).

Fourth, keep Psalm 91 before your eyes. Read it often. Memorize it. Meditate on it. Study it in different translations. You will find your fears vanishing as you read it. You will find confidence rising. You will find intimacy growing. You will find safety. You will find peace.

Let us then make the Lord our dwelling place. Let us live in the hiding place of the Most High!

If you have enjoyed this book, please post a review on Amazon, and please check out our thousands of hours of free resources at AskDrBrown.org.

NOTES

PREFACE

1. Michael Brown, "Is the Coronavirus an End-Time
   Biblical Plague?," *Stream*, March 2, 2020, https://
   stream.org/is-the-coronavirus-an-end-time-biblical-
   plague/.

CHAPTER 1

1. Nicholas Kristof, "The Best-Case Outcome for
   the Coronavirus, and the Worst," *New York
   Times*, March 20, 2020, https://www.nytimes.
   com/2020/03/20/opinion/sunday/coronavirus-
   outcomes.html.
2. Kristof, "The Best-Case Outcome for the
   Coronavirus, and the Worst."
3. Berkeley Lovelace Jr., "Up to 150 Million Americans
   Are Expected to Contract the Coronavirus,
   Congressional Doctor Says," CNBC, March 11,
   2020, https://www.cnbc.com/2020/03/11/up-to-150-
   million-americans-are-expected-to-contract-the-
   coronavirus-congressional-doctor-says.html.

4. Bill Bostock, "Harrowing Video From a Hospital at the Center of Italy's Coronavirus Outbreak Shows Doctors Overwhelmed by Critical Patients," Business Insider, March 20, 2020, https://www.businessinsider.com/video-tour-coronavirus-icu-ward-bergamo-italy-worst-apocalyptic-2020-3.

CHAPTER 2

1. "John Wesley's Big Impact on America," Christianity.com, accessed April 6, 2020, https://www.christianity.com/church/church-history/timeline/1701-1800/john-wesleys-big-impact-on-america-11630220.html.
2. "Christian History: The Moravians and John Wesley," *Christianity Today*, accessed April 6, 2020, https://www.christianitytoday.com/history/issues/issue-1/moravians-and-john-wesley.html.
3. Drudge Report, accessed April 6, 2020, http://www.drudgereportarchives.com.
4. Michael L. Brown, *Jezebel's War With America: The Plot to Destroy Our Country and What We Can Do to Turn the Tide* (Lake Mary, FL: FrontLine, 2019).

CHAPTER 3

1. Omri Ron, "Why Do Some Christians Believe Coronavirus Is an Apocalyptic Prophecy?," *Jerusalem Post*, March 26, 2020, https://www.jpost.com/International/Why-do-some-Christians-believe-coronavirus-is-an-apocalyptic-prophecy-622425.
2. Bill Gates, "Responding to Covid-19—A Once-in-a-Century Pandemic?," *New England Journal of Medicine*, February 28, 2020, https://www.nejm.org/doi/full/10.1056/NEJMp2003762?query=RP.

3. Michael Snyder, "Ten 'Plagues' Are Hitting Our Planet Simultaneously," Technical Politics, February 18, 2020, https://www.technicalpolitics.com/articles/michael-snyder-ten-plagues-are-hitting-our-planet-simultaneously/.

4. "Friday, January 24, 2020: Coronavirus Spreads in China as Government Quarantines 25 Million People: Echoes of Plagues Past, Present, and Future," Albert Mohler—The Briefing, accessed April 6, 2020, https://albertmohler.com/2020/01/24/briefing-1-24-20.

5. Robert Bartholomew, "The Chinese Coronavirus Is Not the Zombie Apocalypse," *Psychology Today*, January 27, 2020, https://www.psychologytoday.com/intl/blog/its-catching/202001/the-chinese-coronavirus-is-not-the-zombie-apocalypse.

6. TOI staff, "Netanyahu Urges Gantz to Help Him 'Save Israel' as Nations Sink Like 'Titanics,'" *Times of Israel*, March 21, 2020, https://www.timesofisrael.com/netanyahu-implores-gantz-to-help-him-save-israel-as-nations-sink-like-titanics/.

7. Matt Smethurst, "C. S. Lewis on the Coronavirus," The Gospel Coalition, March 12, 2020, https://www.thegospelcoalition.org/article/cs-lewis-coronavirus/.

CHAPTER 4

1. Dr. Michael L. Brown, "Should the Church Comply With Government Guidelines?," *The Line of Fire With Dr. Michael Brown*, YouTube, March 19, 2020, https://www.youtube.com/watch?v=sgC6jUVIubg&feature=youtu.be.

2. Dr. Michael L. Brown, "When your little girl has chickenpox, do you bring her to the children's church on Sunday...," Twitter, March 21, 2020,

5:15 p.m., https://twitter.com/DrMichaelLBrown/
status/1241473584083673088.

3. Becky Greene, "When my 5 children were very
small we went to church...," Twitter, March 22,
2020, 10:30 p.m., https://twitter.com/Rebecca__
Greene/status/1241915206629982210.

4. Dr. Michael L. Brown, "Should We Lay Hands on
Someone With the Coronavirus?," *The Line of Fire
With Dr. Michael Brown*, YouTube, March 21, 2020,
https://www.youtube.com
/watch?v=wN8VvQzAn78&feature=youtu.be&fbclid
=IwAR2bsCryfoOqgHDs7Gvb1QeKcKh
AtoIPfMZ5ZvGCztetArapTNDq4xbL8hQ.

5. Karen Anne, "I have led 12 hospital
and nursing home teams in Atlanta...,"
Facebook, accessed April 6, 2020, https://
www.facebook.com/DrMichaelBrown/
posts/10156877464610685?comment_
id=10156877803740685&notif_
id=1584931771360800&notif_t=feed_comment.

6. Michael Brown, "Infringement of Our Rights or
Love Your Neighbor as Yourself?," *Christian Post*,
accessed April 6, 2020, https://www.christianpost.
com/voices/infringement-of-our-rights-or-love-your-
neighbor-as-yourself.html.

7. "Virginia Pastor Who Posted About Coronavirus
Being Mass Hysteria Dies of Virus," LOVEBSCOTT,
March 26, 2020, https://www.lovebscott.com/
virginia-pastor-posted-coronavirus-mass-hysteria-
dies-virus.

8. "Tulsa Pastor First Person to Die of Covid-19 in
Oklahoma," KHBS-TV, updated March 19, 2020,
https://www.4029tv.com/article/tulsa-pastor-first-
person-to-die-of-covid-19-in-oklahoma/31788218?f

bclid=IwAR2DSi2PQmPhOgVMQytw7UigJ0SRPlg-
TEBhLMIfe2XFJ_kwtAdHedsPsm8#.

9. Richard Read, "A Choir Decided to Go Ahead
With Rehearsal. Now Dozens of Members Have
COVID-19 and Two Are Dead," *Los Angeles Times*,
March 29, 2020, https://www.latimes.com/world-
nation/story/2020-03-29/coronavirus-choir-outbreak.

10. Dr. Michael L. Brown, "Psalm 91 in Hebrew," *The
Line of Fire With Dr. Michael Brown*, YouTube,
March 12, 2020, https://www.youtube.com/
watch?v=efy9cQ2e9rA.

Chapter 5

1. Jason Horowitz and Emma Bubola, "Italy's
Coronavirus Victims Face Death Alone,
With Funerals Postponed," *New York Times*,
updated March 19, 2020, https://www.nytimes.
com/2020/03/16/world/europe/italy-coronavirus-
funerals.html?auth=login-email&login=email.

2. Horowitz and Bubola, "Italy's Coronavirus Victims
Face Death Alone, With Funerals Postponed."

3. Horowitz and Bubola, "Italy's Coronavirus Victims
Face Death Alone, With Funerals Postponed."

4. Cary Gordon, "Pastor Gordon: Pastoral
Response to the Coronavirus," *Iowa Standard*,
March 20, 2020, https://theiowastandard.
com/pastor-gordon-pastoral-response-to-the-
coronavirus/?fbclid=IwAR2-nuol_Kc9bt64gD-
h7dOMGMPSGJ_sS6jKoX6c54i9UhFdxFxxvprAh7o.

5. Gordon, "Pastor Gordon: Pastoral Response to the
Coronavirus."

6. Andrew P. Napolitano, "Coronavirus Fear Lets
Government Assault Our Freedom in Violation of
Constitution," Fox News, accessed April 6, 2020,

https://www.foxnews.com/opinion/judge-andrew-napolitano-liberty-coronavirus.

7. Joey Hollingsworth, "Gov. Abbott: Churches Not Mentioned in Executive Order Due to 'Freedom of Religion,'" Nexstar Broadcasting, March 19, 2020, https://www.bigcountryhomepage.com/news/gov-abbott-churches-not-mentioned-in-executive-order-due-to-freedom-of-religion/.

8. Brandon Moseley, "Moore: 'Economy Is Destroyed' by 'Tyrants Who Pander Fear in the Place of Faith,'" Alabama Political Reporter, March 20, 2020, https://www.alreporter.com/2020/03/20/moore-economy-is-destroyed-by-tyrants-who-pander-fear-in-the-place-of-faith/.

9. KY Press News Service, "Massie Blasts Coronavirus Precautions; Opponents Blast Massie for Comments," Forward Kentucky, March 17, 2020, https://forwardky.com/massie-blasts-coronavirus-precautions-opponents-blast-massie-for-comments/.

10. Gordon, "Pastor Gordon: Pastoral Response to the Coronavirus."

11. JJ Zelig, "Huge Overreaction and Abuse of Power With Covid-19," Facebook, accessed April 6, 2020, https://www.facebook.com/DrMichaelBrown/posts/10156861941725685?comment_id=10156865693750685&notif_id=1584562645423461&notif_t=feed_comment.

12. Samuel Smith, "Church Services Evacuated, Pastors Arrested in Several Countries Over Gathering Bans," Christian Post, March 26, 2020, https://www.christianpost.com/news/church-services-evacuated-pastors-arrested-in-several-countries-over-gathering-bans.html?uid=07ed4df3d9&utm_source=The+Christian+Post+List&utm_campaign=c3046d6468-

EMAIL_CAMPAIGN_2020_03_26_03_59&utm_
medium=email&utm_term=0_dce2601630-
c3046d6468-4263913.

13. "Losing Liberty Is the Long-Term Crisis," Liberty
Counsel, March 25, 2020, https://lc.org/newsroom/
details/032520-losing-liberty-is-the-longterm-
crisis-1.

14. "Angela Merkel Complains That Trump Is
Destroying the New World Order," PCMD News
May 19, 2019, https://pcmdnews.com/angela-merkel-
complains-that-trump-is-destroying-the-new-world-
order/.

15. Colum Lynch, "Trump's War on the World Order,"
FP, December 27, 2018, https://foreignpolicy.
com/2018/12/27/trumps-war-on-the-world-order/.

16. Charlie Spiering, "Donald Trump Defends Dream
of 'Packed Churches' on Easter Despite Coronavirus
Fight," Breitbart, March 24, 2020, https://www.
breitbart.com/politics/2020/03/24/donald-trump-
defends-dream-of-packed-churches-on-easter-
despite-coronavirus-fight/.

17. Brooke Singman and Matt Leach, "Trump Says New
Coronavirus 'Guidelines' Will Address Potential
Changes to Social Distancing Rules," Fox News,
March 26, 2020, https://www.foxnews.com/politics/
trump-new-coronavirus-guidelines-will-advise-
potential-changes-social-distancing-rules.

18. Cary Gordon, "I have had some folks ask me about
my reference to Romans 13th chapter being misused
to justify the use of moral and doctrinal fallacies
during the present pandemic of the Coronavirus,"
Facebook, March 21, 2020, https://www.facebook.
com/carypastor.gordon/posts/3054225624640900.

CHAPTER 6

1. "*The Day the Earth Stood Still*," Wikipedia, accessed April 7, 2020, https://en.wikipedia.org/wiki/The_Day_the_Earth_Stood_Still.
2. "*The Day the Earth Stood Still*," Wikipedia.
3. Carlie Porterfield, "Florida Megachurch Pastor Arrested for Defying Coronavirus Stay-at-Home Order and Holding Services," *Forbes*, March 31, 2020, https://www.forbes.com/sites/carlieporterfield/2020/03/31/florida-megachurch-pastor-arrested-for-defying-coronavirus-stay-at-home-order-and-holding-services/#4b51e1796ac6.
4. Rodney Howard-Browne, "Coronavirus in Today's Ministry," Free Republic, March 17, 2020, https://www.freerepublic.com/focus/f-chat/3825353/posts?page=1.
5. Howard-Browne, "Coronavirus in Today's Ministry."
6. Howard-Browne, "Coronavirus in Today's Ministry."
7. "Former British Prime Minister Gordon Brown Voices Support of One World Government," Behold Israel, accessed April 7, 2020, https://beholdisrael.org/former-british-prime-minister-gordon-brown-voices-support-of-one-world-government/?fbclid=IwAR0oPfpns2elGYWVaEG5yBd9BjNYIh4V23T71tnu110Z84Mljq-6C0XZQqM.
8. Michael L. Brown, *How Saved Are We?* (Shippensburg, PA: Destiny Image, 1990), 106–107, https://www.amazon.com/How-Saved-Are-Michael-Brown/dp/1560430559.
9. "No More Business as Usual?," BillMuehlenberg.com, March 21, 2020, https://billmuehlenberg.com/2020/03/21/no-more-business-as-usual-2/.

CHAPTER 7

1. James Robison, "A Meaningful Conversation Between James Robison and Pastor Chris Hodges," *Stream*, March 18, 2020, https://stream.org/a-meaningful-conversation-between-james-robison-and-pastor-chris-hodges/.
2. Robison, "A Meaningful Conversation Between James Robison and Pastor Chris Hodges."
3. Michael L. Brown, *Revolution in the Church* (Bellingham, WA: Kirkdale Press, 2012), 37.
4. Wolfgang Simson, "15 Theses," House Church Basics, accessed April 7, 2020, https://housechurch.org/basics/simson_15.html.
5. Simson, "15 Theses."
6. Watchman Nee, "The Normal Christian Church Life," Living Stream Ministry, accessed April 7, 2020, https://www.ministrysamples.org/excerpts/THE-MEETING-PLACE.HTML.
7. Nee, "The Normal Christian Church Life."
8. Brown, *Revolution in the Church*, 55.
9. "Dr. Brown Interviews Pastor Andy Stanley," YouTube, July 2, 2018, https://www.youtube.com/watch?v=C7Jcu03lJso&feature=youtu.be.

CHAPTER 8

1. Joel Fuhrman, *Eat to Live* (New York: Little, Brown and Company, 2011), https://books.google.com/books?id=UZSaR58r_2oC&printsec=frontcover&dq=eat+to+live&hl=en&newbks=1&newbks_redir=0&sa=X&ved=2ahUKEwjQ69r6ptnoAhWym-AKHZLnAnsQ6AEwAHoECAAQAg#v=onepage&q=eat%20to%20live&f=false.
2. Michael L. Brown with Nancy Brown, *Breaking the Stronghold of Food* (Lake Mary, FL: Siloam, 2017), 37, https://www.amazon.com/

Breaking-Stronghold-Food-Addictions-Discovered/
dp/162999099X/ref=sr_1_1?crid=2RLNYJF70OAAV
&keywords=breaking+the+stronghold+of+food&qid
=1585280244&sprefix=breaking+the+strong%2Caps
%2C159&sr=8-1&pldnSite=1.

3. "Cardiovascular Diseases," World Health
Organization, accessed April 8, 2020, https://
www.who.int/health-topics/cardiovascular-
diseases/#tab=tab_1.

4. Kimberly Hickok, "How does the COVID-19
Pandemic Compare to the Last Pandemic?,"
LiveScience, accessed April 8, 2020, https://www.
livescience.com/covid-19-pandemic-vs-swine-flu.
html.

5. "Immune Function," Dr. Fuhrman, accessed
April 7, 2020, https://www.drfuhrman.com/get-
started/health-concerns/73/immune-function?f
bclid=IwAR3QDah7DkpgOSyAdTI-JCuvC7xD5_
OalBvOq0SMPeRL92anQIBkgv9d5Oo.

6. Michael Brown, "A Personal Appeal to My
Christian Ministry Colleagues: Please Guard Your
Health!," *Stream*, March 8, 2020, https://stream.
org/a-personal-appeal-to-my-christian-ministry-
colleagues-please-guard-your-health/.

7. Ryan W. Miller, "Yes, COVID-19 Can Be Serious
for Younger Adults, Too, CDC Report Shows," *USA
Today*, March 19, 2020, https://www.usatoday.com/
story/news/health/2020/03/19/coronavirus-illnesses-
can-serious-young-adults-cdc-report/2874271001/.

8. Andrew Krietz, "6 Florida College Students Test
Positive for Coronavirus," WTSP-TV, March 22,
2020, https://www.wtsp.com/article/news/health/
coronavirus/university-of-tampa-spring-break-
coronavirus-cases/67-183c52fa-1c33-4673-be03-
129ec35d0980.

9. Tommaso Ebhardt, Chiara Remondini, and Marco Bertacche, "99% of Those Who Died From Virus Had Other Illness, Italy Says," Bloomberg, March 18, 2020, https://www.bloomberg.com/news/articles/2020-03-18/99-of-those-who-died-from-virus-had-other-illness-italy-says.

10. *Jerusalem Post* staff, "Israeli Doctor in Italy: No. of Patients Rises but We Get to Everyone," *Jerusalem Post*, March 29, 2020, https://www.jpost.com/International/Israeli-doctor-in-Italy-We-no-longer-help-those-over-60-621856.

11. Jenni Frazer, "Two Ultra-Orthodox Jews Die in London as Coronavirus Shutters Most Communities," *Times of Israel*, March 22, 2020, https://www.timesofisrael.com/two-ultra-orthodox-jews-die-in-london-as-coronavirus-shutters-most-communities/.

12. "Alfred Gruenther," Wikipedia, updated March 3, 2020, https://en.wikipedia.org/wiki/Alfred_Gruenther.

13. Allana Akhtar and Marguerite Ward, "WeWork Has Turned to a 57-Year Old Real Estate Veteran to Help Turn It Around, Suddenly Becoming the Latest Example of a Spike in Older CEOs Getting Hired," Business Insider, accessed April 8, 2020, https://webcache.googleusercontent.com/search?q=cache:xZZZoyghv7UJ:https://www.businessinsider.com/corporate-america-ceos-are-getting-older-mostly-white-2019-10+&cd=3&hl=en&ct=clnk&gl=us&client=safari.

14. Greg Auman, "How Much Does Age Matter When Hiring NFL Head Coaches?," The Athletic, January 7, 2019, https://theathletic.com/754389/2019/01/07/how-much-does-age-matter-when-hiring-nfl-head-coaches/.

CHAPTER 9

1. Harold J. Chadwick, in Frank "JJ" Di Pietro, *The Fire That Once Was* (Hazel Crest, IL: Penoaks Publishing, 2017), https://www.amazon.com/Fire-That-Once-Was-Turned-ebook/dp/B01NBYIEEZ/ref=sr_1_1?dch ild=1&qid=1586370922&refinements=p_27%3AFrank +%22JJ%22+Di+Pietro&s=digital-text&sr=1-1&text=F rank+%22JJ%22+Di+Pietro.
2. "Ignatius of Antioch," AZ Quotes, accessed April 8, 2020, https://www.azquotes.com/quote/1404895.
3. Di Pietro, *The Fire That Once Was.*
4. Di Pietro, *The Fire That Once Was.*
5. Scott Nary, "My whole life I've been a fighter," Facebook, March 22, 2020, https://www.facebook.com/scott.nary.7/posts/10220593276038059.
6. Bill Muehlenberg, "Faith in a Time of Crisis," CultureWatch, March 23, 2020, https://billmuehlenberg.com.
7. Muehlenberg, "Faith in a Time of Crisis."
8. Muehlenberg, "Faith in a Time of Crisis."
9. Charles Spurgeon, "Psalm 91," The Spurgeon Archive, accessed April 8, 2020, http://www.romans45.org/spurgeon/treasury/ps091.htm.
10. John G. Lake, "The Law of Life and Law of Death," Healing Rooms Ministries, accessed April 8, 2020, https://healingrooms.com/?src=johnglake&docu ment=143.
11. Lake, "The Law of Life and Law of Death."

CHAPTER 10

1. Kyle Mantyla, "Rick Wiles Says Coronavirus Death of LGBTQ Lawyer Is a Sign of God's Judgment," Right Wing Watch, March 23, 2020, https://www.rightwingwatch.org/post/rick-wiles-says-coronavirus-death-of-lgbtq-lawyer-is-a-sign-of-gods-

judgment/?fbclid=IwAR0BVm5JSQ_RClDFnv2is_
N7bfbYvhn_z0VGNeB73KEfQ91KoVPMxbeiVQQ.

2. Nicole Darrah, "Trump's Bible Study Teacher
Claims 'Coronavirus Is God's Punishment for Gay
People and Environmentalism,'" *U.S. Sun*, March
25, 2020, https://www.the-sun.com/news/589777/
donald-trump-ralph-dollinger-coronavirus-bible-
study-minister/.

3. Darrah, "Trump's Bible Study Teacher Claims
'Coronavirus Is God's Punishment for Gay People
and Environmentalism.'"

4. Jeremy Sharon, "Religious Leaders: Coronavirus
Is Punishment, Sign of the Messiah's Coming,"
Jerusalem Post, March 17, 2020, https://www.jpost.
com/international/religious-leaders-coronavirus-is-
punishment-sign-of-the-messiahs-coming-621339.

5. "Is God Judging America Today?," Capitol Ministries,
March 23, 2020, https://www.documentcloud.org/
documents/6818524-Is-God-Judging-America-
Today-by-Ralph-Drollinger.html.

6. Megan Sheets, "Seventeen-year-old in New Orleans
becomes the second child to die of coronavirus in
the US this week as the city prepares to become
the new US epicenter with a spike of 510 infections
in a day," DailyMail.com, updated March 27, 2020,
https://www.dailymail.co.uk/news/article-8157769/
Seventeen-year-old-dies-coronavirus-New-Orleans-
Louisiana-sees-510-new-cases-24-hours.html.

7. Christina Darnell, "Shepherd's Conference
Notification of COVID-19 Death Raises
Questions," Ministry Watch, March 24, 2020,
https://ministrywatch.com/shepherds-conference-
notification-of-covid-19-death-raises-questions/.

8. Leonardo Blair, "Coronavirus Strikes Pastor, Wife
and Over 30 Others at Ark. Church," *Christian Post*,

March 24, 2020, https://www.christianpost.com/news/coronavirus-strikes-pastor-wife-and-over-30-others-at-arkansas-church.html.

9. "What Is God Saying in the Midst of This Pandemic and Quarantine?," Charisma Podcast Network, accessed April 8, 2020, https://www.charismapodcastnetwork.com/show/strangreport/dfeb1fc1-d2fd-4551-9554-88e7bb2c782f.

10. "'Prophet': Coronavirus Sent by God to Convert People to Christianity," Patheos, March 25, 2020, https://www.patheos.com/blogs/dispatches/2020/03/25/prophet-coronavirus-sent-by-god-to-convert-people-to-christianity/.

11. Peter Montgomery, "Lou Engle Calls for Three-Day Fast to Stop Coronavirus and Save Stadium Prayer Rallies," Right Wing Watch, March 20, 2020, https://www.rightwingwatch.org/post/lou-engle-calls-for-three-day-fast-to-stop-coronavirus-and-save-stadium-prayer-rallies/.

12. "The Coronavirus Did Not Escape From a Lab: Here's How We Know," Fox News, accessed April 8, 2020, https://www.foxnews.com/science/the-coronavirus-did-not-escape-from-a-lab-heres-how-we-know.

13. My Facebook page is https://www.facebook.com/AskDrBrown/posts/4290077951017774?__tn__=-R; Twitter is https://twitter.com/DrMichaelLBrown/status/1242856149696876545.

14. "COVID-19: Get the Latest Information from the CDC About COVID-19," *The Line of Fire*, YouTube, accessed April 8, 2020, https://www.youtube.com/watch?v=sIbRL3CBzNE&feature=youtu.be.

15. "Have Faith!," YouTube, March 25, 2020, https://www.youtube.com/watch?v=bsj0OAdloag&feature=youtu.be.

16. "10 Contrasts Between True Christ Followers and the World During a Crisis," Joseph Mattera, March 25, 2020, https://josephmattera.org/10-contrasts-between-true-christ-followers-and-the-world-during-a-crisis/.

17. "Catherine Booth Quotes," QuoteFancy, accessed April 8, 2020, https://quotefancy.com/catherine-booth-quotes.

CHAPTER 11

1. Robert Nicholson, "A Coronavirus Great Awakening?," *Wall Street Journal*, March 26, 2020, https://www.wsj.com/articles/a-coronavirus-great-awakening-11585262324.

2. Nicholson, "A Coronavirus Great Awakening?"

CHAPTER 12

1. "Psalm 91 Bible Commentary: Charles H. Spurgeon's Treasury of David," Christianity.com, accessed April 8, 2020, https://www.christianity.com/bible/commentary.php?com=spur&b=19&c=91.